performance

Bloomsbury Movie Guides

mick brown *on*

performance

pocket movie guide 6

BLOOMSBURY

First published in Great Britain 1999
This edition published 2000

Copyright © 1999 by Mick Brown

The moral right of the author has been asserted

Bloomsbury Publishing Plc, 38 Soho Square, London, W1V 5DF

A CIP catalogue record for this book
is available from the British Library

ISBN 0 7475 5191 X

10 9 8 7 6 5 4 3 2 1

Typeset by Palimpsest Book Production Limited,
Polmont, Stirlingshire
Printed in Great Britain by Clays Limited, St Ives plc

Introduction

'I always thought *Performance* was a comedy.'

Donald Cammell

I first saw *Performance* in 1972, a year after its British release, in the Electric, a small repertory cinema in Notting Hill. Enhanced, no doubt, by the overpowering aroma of hashish wafting around the cinema (an essential element of any visit to the Electric in those days), the primary effect was sensory. *Performance* presented a rich and dazzling brocade of sexual licence, hallucinogenic pleasures, pulsating rock and roll – and a voyeuristic *frisson* of violence – a thrilling portrait of a London which I recognised, and yearned to know better, with its intimation of exotic and forbidden pleasures. I can still remember stepping out into the Portobello Road, stunned and exhilarated and disturbed, this mixture of sensations immeasurably heightened by the knowledge that the house in Powis Square where the rock star Turner and his girlfriend Pherber had, just a few moments before, been so artfully disarranging the mind of the gangster Chas, was but a few minutes' walk away.

I have lost count of the number of times I have seen the film since then, but on every occasion it seems to have offered some fresh revelation. *Performance* is not just a film which repays repeated viewing, it demands it; like a mandala, its surface imagery, hypnotically dazzling in itself, actually contains a myriad of more subtle meanings and resonances.

Performance is a film that, as Marianne Faithfull memorably put it, 'preserves a whole era under glass', freeze-framing London at the tail end of the Sixties: the London of the Rolling Stones and of the Kray twins, of newly found sexual freedom, drug-drenched hedonism and psychopathic violence.

Superficially a 'crime movie about rock and roll' – which is how the idea of the film was first sold to Warner Bros – *Performance* is a multi-textured feast for the mind and the senses; a film which simultaneously explores the nature of identity, the relationship between violence and creativity, sex and death, organised crime, amorality, power, drugs, and rock and roll. As Turner, the rock-star anti-hero (played by Mick Jagger), says at one point in the film: 'The only performance that makes it, that really makes it, that makes it all the way, is the one that achieves madness.' And *Performance* is about that too.

Technically speaking, in its use of fast cuts, flash backs, flash forwards or flashes of seemingly unrelated events happening simultaneously – its sense of time not so much suspended as completely disarrayed – the film was truly pioneering. Its use of music was equally ground-breaking: the 'Memo From Turner' sequence stands as arguably the first fully-fledged rock video, a perfect integration of film and music.

But it is the film's dazzling integration of themes –

shaped by the cultural and sexual obsessions of its author, Donald Cammell, and by his prodigious intelligence and imagination – which makes *Performance* so extraordinary; and it is the circumstances which surrounded the film – the story behind the story – which make it the cult movie nonpareil.

Even before its opening in Britain in January 1971 the film had acquired its own peculiar mythology. Shot in the summer of 1968, *Performance* sat on the shelf for more than two years while Warner Bros deliberated on whether or not to release it, so disturbed were they by the film's treatment of drugs-use and sexuality. And just as *Performance* is a film that seems, in some curious way, to leave an indelible mark on everyone who sees it, so it is also a film that seems to have for ever changed those who were associated with it. James Fox, then a rising star in Britain and Hollywood, was allegedly so disturbed by the events of the film that shortly afterwards he retired from acting altogether and took to Christian evangelism. He did not work again for ten years. Anita Pallenberg left the set of *Performance* addicted to heroin. Michèle Breton fell into a life of drug-addiction, destitution and mental breakdown. Mick Jagger emerged apparently unscathed, but within a year unleashed the demon that was Altamont. For Donald Cammell, *Performance*'s writer, co-director and presiding alchemist, the film would cast a baleful shadow over his life and career that would come to horrific fruition some thirty years later. The one obvious beneficiary was Cammell's co-director, Nicolas Roeg, for whom the movie acted as the first step in what would become a distinguished film career.

* * *

Performance falls into two quite distinct sections. The first seems to be setting the film up as crime thriller – albeit a fairly unconventional one. Chas Devlin (James Fox) is an East End hood, an enforcer for the racketeer Harry Flowers (Johnny Shannon). The film begins by establishing the nature of Chas's particular craft, and of the man. We see him engaging in a bout of frantic, sado-masochistic – and distinctly self-absorbed – sex with his night-club-singer girlfriend, Dana, then setting off for a day's work with his fellow thugs Rosebloom ('Rosie') and Moody, putting the frighteners on a mini-cab firm and a Soho blue-movie exhibitor. These scenes are intercut with a courtroom sequence in which a barrister is threatening to drag Harry Flowers's name into a court-case involving a former business associate. Chas, Moody and Rosebloom intercept the barrister and his client outside a gentleman's club, and threaten them both. When the barrister tells Chas to 'address your remarks to me', Chas takes him at his word. The next morning they ambush the barrister's chauffeur, brutally shave his head and pour acid over the barrister's Rolls-Royce.

This bit of business duly dealt with, Harry Flowers now turns his attention to another – the 'acquisition' of a betting-shop owned by an erstwhile friend of Chas's, Joey Maddocks. Clearly bent on settling some private vendetta, Chas eagerly volunteers for the job of wrecking the betting-shop. Instead, Flowers assigns the task to Rosebloom and forbids Chas to have anything to do with it. The next day, however, it is Chas who collects Maddocks from the wreckage of his betting-shop and delivers him to Flowers in a Soho drinking-club. His initiative incurs the wrath of Flowers ('Who do you think you are? The bleeding Lone Ranger?') and leads to Chas being ambushed in his flat and viciously beaten by Maddocks and two heavies in reprisal. During the attack Chas manages to struggle free and shoots Maddocks dead. A dangerous embarrassment to 'the Firm', wanted by both Flowers and the police, Chas goes on the run. He telephones his mother, who suggests that he hides out with an aunt in Barnstaple, Devon. In the buffet of Paddington railway station, he overhears a musician talking about a basement flat which is available for rent in the Powis Square house of a reclusive rock star, Turner (Mick Jagger).

Chas makes his way to Turner's home, and posing, improbably, as 'Johnny Dean', a night-club juggler in town for a series of engagements – 'all A1 venues' – he inveigles his way into the house.

From the moment that Chas steps across the threshold of 81 Powis Square, *Performance* enters a quite different, altogether more hallucinatory realm. Turner has long ago lost his creative impetus and now whiles away the days with his lover Pherber (Anita Pallenberg) and a French waif, Lucy (Michèle Breton), in a listless round of sex and drugs, tended by the motherly, and curiously broad-minded, Mrs Gibbs and her precocious young daughter Laraine.

Chas telephones a friend, Tony, and instructs him to make arrangements for passage to America by cargo ship, then turns his thoughts to consolidating a new identity to make good his escape.

From the outset, it is clear that neither Pherber nor Turner believes Chas's story that he is a night-club juggler, but Turner recognises in Chas – a man who makes his living from violence and intimidation, who physically embodies violence – the 'demon' that he has lost in himself and agrees to let him stay. Playing along with Chas's need for a passport-photo, Pherber and Turner begin to play first with his appearance and then with his mind, dissolving his identity – his 'performance' – in a crucible of hallucinogenic drugs and sexuality.

Completely disorientated, Chas makes another, belated, call to Tony, to arrange for him to collect the passport-photo. Unaware that Rosebloom and Moody are sitting in Tony's bedroom as he takes the call, Chas lets slip the address of Turner's house. Transformed now by his encounter with Turner and Pherber, Chas makes love to Lucy with a tenderness that has been wholly absent from his character until now.

The next morning, he prepares to leave for refuge in America, but in the hallway he is confronted by Rosebloom and his cronies. Realising that he is about to meet his death, Chas walks upstairs for his final encounter with Turner. Turner tells Chas he wants to come with him. 'You don't know where I'm going,' says Chas. 'Yes I do,' Turner replies. Chas calmly draws his gun and shoots Turner through the head. The camera follows the bullet as it spirals into Turner's cerebral cortex, then tracks out of the house to a neighbouring rooftop where a gunman stands guard, and down to the street, where, from behind, we see the figure of Chas being led towards Harry Flowers's white Rolls-Royce.

Rosebloom, meanwhile, gives the house a final once-over. He opens a cupboard to reveal the bloodstained body of Turner, lying among some old picture frames.

Outside, we see the figure of Chas climbing into the Rolls-Royce and being greeted by Harry Flowers – 'Hello Chas.' As the car pulls away, Chas turns to look out of the car window and we see that he now has Turner's face. The two men have become one.

'The film is simply about an idea,' Donald Cammell told the film-critic Derek Malcolm in an interview published in the *Guardian* in 1970, shortly before the British release of *Performance*. 'It's a movie that gets into an allegorical area and it moves from a definition of what violence is to an explanation of a way of being. It is an attempt, maybe successful and maybe not, to use a film for exploring the nature of violence as seen from the point of view of an artist. It says that this crook leads this fading pop star to realise that violence is a facet of creative art, that his energy is derived from the same sources of those as the crook. And that that energy is always dangerous, sometimes fatal.'

Performance took its spirit from the London milieu of which its director and principal players were all a part: the intersection at which the worlds of rock music, the new aristocracy – and crime – collided. Marianne Faithfull would describe it as 'an allegory of libertine Chelsea life in the late 60s, with its baronial rock stars, wayward *jeunesse dorée*, drugs, sex and decadence'.

It was a film galvanised by the relationships, both on and off screen, of its principals. Cammell, Fox and Jagger were all close friends. Cammell had lived in *ménages à trois*, at different times, with both Anita Pallenberg and Michèle Breton. At the time of making the film, Pallenberg was the lover of Keith Richard, Jagger's fellow Rolling Stone and closest friend. It is this intermingling of relationships that has led to *Performance* being described, with some justification, as 'the most expensive home movie ever made'.

The film was sold to Warner Bros on the basis of a skimpy treatment about a chance meeting between a rock star and a gangster. There was no proper script: Cammell hadn't written one. He began the film not knowing how it would end, and would later claim that even halfway through shooting he had no clear idea who would live and who would die.

Cammell had scripted two films before *Performance* but had no experience as a director. Nor did his co-director, Nic Roeg, although he was an experienced and highly respected cinematographer. *Performance* was also the first film for its producer, Sanford 'Sandy' Lieberson. It is difficult to imagine any major film company these days allowing such an inexperienced team the degree of freedom which Warner afforded Lieberson, Cammell and Roeg in 1968. Warner's willingness to forgo the normal checks and balances can only be understood in the context of the times. While it had been a full three years since *Time* magazine had decreed London as 'swinging', the myth was still abroad in Hollywood (and hard though it may be to believe, Warner thought *Performance* was going to be a 'Swinging London' film). The success of the Beatles' films *Help* and *A Hard Day's Night* had made pop stars a valuable commercial commodity in film as well as music. And Mick Jagger was the biggest rock star of the day, bar none. (Such was Warner's enthusiasm for Jagger that they attempted to contract him as a 'youth advisor' to the company on the back of the *Performance* deal. The proposal was quietly dropped when the film was completed.) In short, Warner thought it was getting a 'youth market' movie, but was unprepared for one that actually reflected the more extreme tastes, mores and enthusiasms of that market.

Only after filming had begun did Warner executives begin to express doubts about the film's volatile contents, their nervousness increasing almost by the day, to the point where filming was actually halted and the fate of the project hung in the balance. When, at last, the film was delivered to the studio it was received with shudders of apprehension. At a test screening in Santa Monica members of the audience walked out of the theatre in protest. Legend has it that the wife of one studio executive actually threw up. Warner Bros refused to release the film without substantial cuts and re-editing, and it was to be two years before it was eventually released for public exhibition. By that time its cult-status was already assured.

Performance was given its world première in New York on 30 July 1970, heralded by an advertisement in the *Village Voice* showing pictures of Jagger in rock-star and gangster guise, alongside copy which read: 'Somewhere in your head there's a wild electric dream. Come see it in *Performance*, where underground meets underworld.'

The film was greeted by cries of bewilderment and outrage from critics. John Simon, writing in the *New York Times*, wondered if it wasn't 'the most loathsome film of all', while Andrew Sarris in the *Village Voice* described it as 'the most deliberately decadent film I have ever seen'. Both *Rolling Stone* magazine in America and the British underground newspaper *IT* saw fit to offer public health warnings, cautioning their readers not to watch *Performance* while tripping on LSD.

Extraordinarily, the intervening years have done nothing to diminish the impact of *Performance*. It remains as dazzling, provocative and thought-provoking now as it did thirty years ago – a film which traps 'a whole era under glass' certainly, but which transcends the age in which it was made by virtue of its singularity and its brilliance, and which has continued to exercise a powerful fascination on successive generations as one of the greatest British films, of any kind, of all time.

A

Artaud, Antonin (1896–1948)

As Chas floats in an hallucinogenic haze, Turner steps from the shadows to utter what is perhaps *Performance*'s most memorable and resonant line: 'The only performance that makes it, that really makes it, that makes it all the way, is the one that achieves madness.'

The words are a homage to Antonin Artaud, the French writer, actor, director and artist whose work and ideas Cammell so much admired, and who can be regarded as one of abiding spirits which hovered over the creation of *Performance*.

Artaud's principal legacy was his theories on 'The Theatre of Cruelty', in which he argued that performance as a passive spectacle should be abandoned in favour of a sensory and intellectual bombardment through which the audience would be shocked out of its complacency and moved to states of spiritual transcendence. 'I employ the word cruelty in the sense of an appetite for life,' he wrote, 'an implacable necessity, in the gnostic sense of a living whirlwind that devours darkness.'

Artaud lived his whole life in a traumatic journey back and forth across the boundary between sanity and madness. At the age of four he contracted meningitis and was 'treated' by a primitive form of electro-shock therapy that left its legacy in headaches, facial tics and mood swings that would haunt him throughout his youth. At the age of eighteen, he suffered his first nervous breakdown, and spent the next five years undergoing 'rest cures' at a variety of clinics and spas in France and Switzerland, culminating in a doctor prescribing opium, to which he would remain addicted for the rest of his life.

By now, Artaud had begun to draw and write, incorporating poetry, prose, chants and word-fragments into a singular manifesto of self. Briefly involved with the Surrealists (he was expelled by André Breton over his protest against the movement aligning itself with the Communist party), Artaud concentrated on writing and performing for the theatre, supplementing his income with film appearances (among them, roles in Abel Gance's *Napoleon* and Carl Dreyer's *La Passion de Jeanne d'Arc*).

It was his mounting frustration with the conventions of performance, and the boundary between the spectactor and the spectacle, which led him to devise the first Theatre of Cruelty manifesto in 1932, arguing for an abandonment of narrative and structure – even of language – in favour of a drama of ritualistic gesture, sound and music – a sensory attack to shock the audience into wakefulness. 'They do not realise they are dead.'

Artaud's theories were greeted with widespread incomprehension and hostility and his attempts to translate his ideas to the stage were predictable failures, exacerbating his chronic destitution and his ever-fragile mental condition. 'I abandoned the stage,' he later explained, 'because I realised the fact that the only language which I could have with an audience was to bring bombs out of my pockets and throw them in the audience's face with a blatant gesture of aggression . . . and blows are the only language in which I feel capable of speaking.'

After a series of journeys to Mexico (where he took part in peyote ceremonies with local Indians) and Ireland (from where he was deported after claiming to speak with the voice of God), he was admitted to a mental institution in France. He was to spend the next nine years undergoing a variety of treatments, including coma-inducing insulin therapy and some fifty electro-shock treatments, all the while remaining coherent enough to write a series of letters to his doctors pleading with them to stop. Artaud would later argue that madness was the honourable choice in a society devoid of honour, and that psychiatric treatment was a way of punishing dissent from society's norms.

His last major work, a year after his release from the mental institution in 1946, was a radiophonic creation entitled *To Have Done With the Judgement of God* – a feverish and scatological attack on a variety of subjects including America and the Catholic Church, in which excrement is exalted as the stuff of life and God appears as a dissected organ wrenched from the defective corpse of mankind. Banned at the last moment, the programme was subsequently broadcast thirty years after Artaud's death.

He continued to write up to the moment of his death, from liver cancer. His last, scribbled fragment read:

And they have pushed me over
into death
where I ceaselessly eat

cock
anus
and caca
at all my meals,
all those of THE CROSS.

B

Bacon, Francis (1909–92)

English painter, habitué of London's Colony Room club, acquaintance of the Kray twins and David Litvinoff. Bacon's powerful, and sometimes grotesque and disturbing portraiture could be seen as an existentialist cry of anguish in a Godless world – representing his view, expressed shortly before his death, that: 'We are born and we die and there's nothing else. We're just part of animal life.'

Donald Cammell and Nicolas Roeg paid homage to Bacon in the concluding shot in the 'Memo From Turner' sequence, where the camera pans back to reveal the naked bodies of Rosebloom, Moody and Dennis intertwined on the floor. The shapes of the recumbent figures and the dramatic use of light and shade are clearly inspired by Bacon's work.

It is not known whether Cammell and Bacon ever met, but Bacon's life in the bohemian, artistic and homosexual *demi-monde* would no doubt have been of interest to Cammell. In his book *The Gilded Gutter Life of Francis Bacon*, Daniel Farson amusingly recounts a meeting in Tangier between Bacon and the beat authors William Burroughs and Allen Ginsberg, when Burroughs attempted to turn Bacon on to kif and the painter's face 'blew up like a balloon' because of his asthma.

Farson writes that: 'Allen Ginsberg described Francis at that period as a satyr with the looks of an English schoolboy who "wears sneakers and tight dungarees and black silk shirts and always looks like going to tennis . . . and paints mad gorillas in grey hotel rooms dressed in evening dress with deathly black umbrellas – said he would paint a big pornographic picture of me & Peter [Orlovsky]".'

Barber

Rosebloom's old man wasn't one. Shut your hole, Moody!

Beaton, Cecil (1904–80)

The celebrated fashion and social photographer and diarist Cecil Beaton made several appearances on the set of *Performance* in Lowndes Square to take stills photographs.

Beaton was commissioned by Sandy Lieberson, whose then wife, Marit Allen, worked for *Vogue* magazine and was a friend of the photographer. Warner refused to pay for Beaton's services, so Lieberson paid the fee out of his own pocket.

Beaton was much taken with Mick Jagger, following his first encounter with the singer at the Mamounia Hotel in Marrakesh in 1967, where the Stones had fled after the Redlands bust (see **Mars Bars**). Beaton's first impressions of Jagger later found their way into Philip Norman's definitive biography of the group, *The Stones*.

On the Tuesday evening I came down to dinner very late and, to my surprise, sitting in the hotel lobby discovered Mick Jagger and a sleepy-looking band of gypsies . . . I didn't want to give the impression that I was only interested in Mick, but it happened that we sat next to one another as he drank a Vodka Collins and smoked with pointed finger held high. His skin is chicken-breast white and of a fine quality. He has an inborn elegance . . . We went to a Moroccan restaurant. Mick . . . is very gentle and with perfect manners. He has much appreciation and his small, albino-fringed eyes notice everything. He has an analytical slant and compares everything he is seeing here with earlier impressions in other countries.

He asked: 'Have you ever taken LSD? Oh I should. It would mean so much to you; you'd never forget the colours. For a painter it's a great experience. One's brain works not on four cylinders but on four thousand.'

[The next morning] I took Mick through the trees to photograph him in the midday sun . . . He is sexy, yet completely sexless. He could nearly be a eunuch. As a model he is a natural.

Beaton was sixty-three when he became enamoured with the Stones. The essayist Cyril Connolly, reflecting on Beaton's infatuation with all things pop, acerbically dubbed him 'Rip Van Withit'.

In the Beginning . . .

In 1967, energised and excited by England's burgeoning cultural and sexual revolution, Donald Cammell moved

to London from Paris, where he had been living for two
years, writing film scripts.

For Cammell, the catalyst was the Rolling Stones. He
had first become acquainted with Brian Jones through
Anita Pallenberg, a close friend of Cammell's girlfriend
of the time, Deborah Dixon. Cammell was somewhat
older than the Stones, but he was fascinated by Jones and
his circle. The cultural explosion of 'Swinging London'
had already become old news, but it had left enduring
social changes in its wake. In a certain area of British
life at least, the traditional class divisions had been melted
in the crucible of rock music, drugs and newly found
sexual freedom. The London in which Donald Cammell
immersed himself was a world in which the new aristocracy of working-class pop stars rubbed shoulders with
the wayward children of the aristocracy of peers and
landowners. It was a world that encompassed the 'old
bohemia' of the Colony Room club in Soho (where the
painter Francis Bacon held court) and the Chelsea set (of
which Cammell himself had been a part in the Fifties) –
an interlocking network of *jeunesse dorée* pop stars, artists,
debs, aristo-chancers, upper-class drug-dabblers and, when
the *frisson* of danger was required, the newly glamorous world of organised crime. The Kray twins, who
ran protection rackets in the East End and the West
End, were occasionally to be seen at the Ad Lib and
the Scotch of St James and received the imprimatur
of fashionable notoriety when they were photographed
by David Bailey for his book of portraits of the mov-
ers and shakers of Sixties London, *Goodbye Baby and
Amen*.

The Krays were a source of particular fascination to Cammell. In Paris, he had become enamoured of the transgressive literature of William Burroughs and Jean Genet, the homosexual jail-bird whose novels portrayed criminals as existentialist heroes. The seedy glamour of the Krays provided a local counterpoint to Genet's romantic vision of the criminal. 'The mixture of comedy and cruelty' of the gangster's world, Cammell would later explain, 'was the stuff of life at that time.'

The designer and dandy Christopher Gibbs would later remember it as a time of 'tremendous, unequalled social fluidity. Music was one of the levellers, hashish another. It was a bohemian world: Soho, the old *nostalgie de la boue*, and the upper-crust fascination with the criminal world.' Certainly hedonistic, says Gibbs, 'but quite high-minded. It was quite fine. It wasn't coarse. And people were warm and amusing and accommodating rather than pompous.'

The particular circle in which Cammell moved revolved, to a large extent, around Brian Jones's flat at 1 Courtfield Road, Earls Court; Robert Fraser's Cork Street gallery, and the Indica bookshop. Its constituent members were Jones and his girlfriend Anita Pallenberg; Mick Jagger; Marianne Faithfull; Robert Fraser; Christopher Gibbs; the photographer Michael Cooper; Suna Portman; the Ormsby-Gores; Kenneth Anger, the American underground film-maker and occultist, and the Guinness heir Tara Browne, whose death in a car accident was famously memorialised in Lennon and McCartney's 'A Day in the Life'.

Performance would capture perfectly the prevailing mood

of this milieu: the easy hedonism; the sense of gradual corruption and decay – hothouse flowers wilting in the heat of excess and sycophancy. It is a mood vividly illustrated in Marianne Faithfull's autobiography, where she tells of an evening at Jones's Courtfield Road flat, which is rudely interrupted by the arrival on the doorstep of his abandoned inamorata, Linda, clutching Jones's son Julian in her arms and begging for money. Faithfull describes Jones and Anita Pallenberg peering down from the balcony at the unfortunate mother and child 'as if they were some inferior species', roaring with laughter.

From this social milieu, and from his interest in rock music, the new sexual politics and crime, the seeds of *Performance* began to take shape in Donald Cammell's mind:

> I was interested in the idea of an artist at the end of the road. I wanted to write something about an artist in that predicament. It could have been any kind of artist; a painter, a writer, a concert pianist. But I had access to the biggest rock and roll singer in the world, and I was interested in that world. And there is no art form in which the violent impulse is more implicit than in rock music. And I was very interested in what was happening with Mick at that time, the flirtation with Their Satanic Majesties.

Among Cammell's friends in London was Sandy Lieberson, whom he had originally met through Robert Fraser. Lieberson, an American, was working as an agent for Creative Management Artists (CMA), in which capacity he represented the interests of Mick Jagger and the other Rolling Stones for film and television. Another of Lieberson's clients was the actor James Coburn, who had starred with James Fox in the film *Duffy*, which had been scripted by Donald Cammell. On the basis of that script, Lieberson offered to represent Cammell:

> I was terribly impressed by Donald. He was an original in terms of his personality, character, outlook on life. We formed a really close friendship very quickly and talked about movies and what we both wanted to do. At that time, everybody was leaving the agency business to become film producers and I thought, why don't I do that? So Donald and I decided to try and do something together.

The first seeds of what would become *Performance* were contained in a brief treatment which Cammell wrote about the chance meeting in London between an American gangster and a rock star. It was called *The Liars*.

Sandy Lieberson: 'Donald had written a very sketchy treatment and from that we decided to approach Mick and Marlon Brando. Mick was a friend of ours; the Rolling Stones were a superstar group, and Donald and I thought Mick had something rather particular about him that would work in movies. I had met Marlon Brando, and Donald had met him in Paris through [the actor] Christian Marquand. So we thought, wouldn't it be interesting to have Mick Jagger and Marlon Brando in a film. As the idea evolved and the treatment became longer, it was written specifically for Jagger and Brando. It was driven by those two actors, absolutely.

'We submitted *The Liars* to Brando, but he was caught up in doing other things, and it would have meant a lot of courting and a lot of waiting, and we decided that would be unrealistic. So instead we decided to develop it for James Fox, who had become quite friendly with Donald.'

Lieberson suggested that Cammell should direct the film himself – 'God knows why I suggested that, but I did' – but Cammell proposed that he should have a collaborator, the cinematographer Nic Roeg. Cammell had first met Roeg in his days as a Chelsea portrait painter, when Roeg was working as a clapper boy, and they had become good friends. In the intervening years, Roeg had developed an illustrious reputation as a cinematographer.

Sandy Lieberson: 'Donald was smart enough to realise that he knew very little about the practical side of cinema. He had a tremendous interest in cinema, but in terms of his own skills as a film-director I think he felt a little insecure.

'I'd known Nic by reputation, but hadn't met him. I was enormously impressed by him and drawn to him as a person. We had a lunch at the Trattoria Terrazza in Dean Street and we agreed at that point we would all do this together. And I pulled out my diary and said, a good time to start this would probably be July of '68. And I marked it in the diary.'

*   *   *

By that time, Cammell had completed a rough outline of the screenplay. Lieberson approached his former colleagues at CMA, Freddie Fields and David Begelman, to handle the project, and they in turn approached Ken Hyman, the head of production at Warner Bros in London (Hyman's father, Elliott, was chairman of Warner at the time, and Hyman himself had produced *The Dirty Dozen*).

Sandy Lieberson: 'The deal was sold here in London but finalised in California. It was all very vague at that point. In fact, the film was sold, basically, on the basis of Mick Jagger being in it. We hadn't even finalised the budget. Kenny and I knew each other, but he hadn't met Donald. But that was how deals were done in those days. Eventually we drew up a budget of £1.1m, including contingency.

'It was a very modest budget, but even so, Warners were very nervous about it. It was very unusual for people to co-direct films, I think they'd have preferred Nic to direct, Donald to write. They were saying, "At least Nic's had some industry experience, he's a lighting cameraman and so on."' But I insisted it was a partnership and that was it. Nic would never have dumped Donald anyway.

'Warners had a production supervisor, Raymond Anzarat. He was a meticulous man in terms of budget and scheduling and everything like that. He thought it was absolutely ludicrous that Warners had approved the film. Nic and Donald had never directed a film before. I'd never produced a film before. We were producing it out of some office in Chelsea. It couldn't have been further from conventional movie making. He loathed the fact that we were making this film, and making it this way. And he wrote me endless memos berating us about how unprofessional we were, the script was terrible, the budget was unrealistic.

'Looked at from today's perspective, it seems like a miracle that it ever got made at all. But you've got to remember the times. There was a feeling then that almost anything would get a green light in England. It was the peak of Swinging London. *Performance* was just one of a whole bevy of movies that was approved through a spirit of euphoric optimism about what was going to come out of England. It was a very special moment in history. I've never seen it anywhere else, and it never happened again. And you certainly couldn't make a movie like that now. Absolutely not.

'But we weren't making a film "in the tradition" of anything; we were doing something completely different. It was like a glorious game, because at that time in London in the late Sixties there was a group of people who hung out together, who had mutual interests, whatever those interests might be. We were in each other's beds, so to speak, continually. There was this continuous thing of Anita and Mick and Keith and Donald and myself and David Litvinoff and Robert Fraser and Christopher Gibbs. We always saw each other. And some of it was to do with the movie, but most of it was on a personal basis. It was the feeling that was going on in London at that time. And that was just projected on to the screen.'

See also **William Burroughs, Jean Genet, Christopher Gibbs, Kray Twins**.

Bindon, John (1943–93)

John Bindon was amply qualified to play the role of Chas's henchman, Moody. A man who moved between the worlds of show-business and crime, Bindon was a familiar face on cinema and television screens in the Sixties and Seventies, usually cast in the role of the 'heavy', but he also served time in a variety of penal institutions, and once stood trial at the Old Bailey on a murder charge. Indeed, in the absence of his own script, Cammell could have done worse than simply to film Bindon's life-story as an example of the different facets of 'performance'.

The son of a taxi driver, Bindon was born and grew up in Fulham, West London, where, as a young boy, he earned the nickname 'Biffo' because of his volatile temperament. At the age of eleven, he was charged with malicious damage. A few years later he was sent to Borstal for possession of live ammunition.

Bindon occupied himself in a variety of odd jobs, including plucking pheasants, laying asphalt, unloading barges and dealing in antiques, until making a fortuitous break into film in 1966, playing opposite Carol White in Ken Loach's film of Nell Dunn's book *Poor Cow*. Loach had overheard Bindon holding court in a West London pub and decided he would be perfect for the film. 'The only thing out of character,' Bindon later said of his role, 'is that I have to hit Carol White in one scene – and I never hit women.'

The success of the film launched Bindon on a new career as an actor. As well as *Performance*, he played roles in *Quadrophenia*, and John Huston's film *The Macintosh Man*, and had a variety of minor parts in TV series such as *Z Cars*, *Hazell* and *The Sweeney*.

Talking of Bindon's role in *Performance*, Nic Roeg described him as a 'wild, naked talent; an extraordinary man; a totally unafraid person. People often mistrust that, mistake it for pugnacity ... I liked his attitude of raw courage; he had an unencumbered attitude – people are so often encumbered by fear.'

As if to confirm Roeg's opinion, in the same year he made *Performance* Bindon won the Queen's Award for bravery, after rescuing a drowning man from the Thames, although it was later alleged that Bindon himself had pushed the man in the water, and only jumped in to save him when a policeman appeared.

Bindon's growing celebrity and ebulliently extrovert character made him a popular figure in show-business and café-society circles, an amusing 'bit of rough', whose favourite party trick was to balance six half-pint beer mugs on his penis. In 1968 he was taken up by Vicki Hodge, a baronet's daughter turned model, who invited him to Mustique, where Bindon allegedly charmed Princess Margaret – but Bindon, it seems, could charm anyone. His agent, Tony Howard, described him as 'a genial fellow, welcome everywhere he went, from the highest to the lowest places. He could make a horse laugh ...' He also enjoyed affairs with Christine Keeler and Angie Bowie. But Bindon could not keep out of trouble. As the acting work dried up, he was alleged to be earning money from running protection rackets in Fulham and Chelsea, but by 1976 he was declared bankrupt.

A year later he was working as a bodyguard for Led Zeppelin, and was involved in a notorious incident at the Oakland Coliseum when he and Zeppelin's manager, Peter Grant, were alleged to have assaulted an employee of the impresario Bill Graham. Bindon was never charged for that assault, but in 1979 he stood trial at the Old Bailey for the murder of Johnny Darke, a gangland figure who was stabbed to death in a fight at the Ranelagh yacht club in Fulham. It was alleged that Bindon had been paid £10,000 to kill Darke. Bindon claimed that he had been pinned to the ground by Darke and had killed him in self-defence. He was acquitted of the charge. Among those to give evidence on his behalf was the actor Bob Hoskins, who had worked with Bindon at the Old Vic, and described him as 'comical, like a big teddy bear'. 'When Bob walked in,' Bindon later recalled, 'the jury knew I was OK.'

But Bindon's life was downhill from then on. An attempt to start his own shoe business was short-lived, and he was convicted of using a piece of paving-stone as an offensive weapon against a 'short and weedy' man, whose sole crime was accidentally to bump into Bindon as he was celebrating his birthday. Further convictions followed – for causing criminal damage in a restaurant and possessing an offensive weapon. Bindon had long since vanished from the screen and the diary columns of newspapers, his party trick apparently no longer in demand. By the time of his death from cancer in 1993, he was penniless and lonely, living on social security in the tiny Belgravia flat which was his sole legacy from happier days.

Black Swan, Effingham Junction, Surrey

The country pub, seen in the film's opening sequence, where, we assume, the barrister Harley-Brown is enjoying an agreeable lunch, while his chauffeur waits outside, polishing his Rolls-Royce.

Borges, Jorge Luis (1899–1986)

The Argentine writer Borges's ideas had a powerful influence on Cammell and his script for *Performance*.

The son of a lawyer and a teacher of psychology, Borges was educated in Geneva, where his family was travelling when the First World War broke out. There he learned French and German and read the work of the German Expressionist poets, some of which he translated into Spanish. He began writing poetry and returned to Buenos Aires in 1921. Borges published three verse collections and half a dozen volumes of literary and philosophical essays before eventually turning to the short story form. In his early tales he began to explore the labyrinthine processes of the mind and the creation of parallel intellectual universes. His vision – influenced by writers like Stevenson, Wells and Chesterton – was basically realistic but usually contained one central fantastic element. He is generally regarded as a forerunner of the school of so-called magic realism which flourished in the Seventies.

Borges held that all fantastic literature was based on one of four essential devices: the work within the work, the contamination of reality by dream, the voyage in time, or the double. Time and again, his stories revolve on themes that dissolve the thin membrane between

reality and illusion. Among other ideas, he toyed with
the notion that 'any man is all men'. He also wrote about
the possibility of the transmigration of the soul and the
congruence of events at different times and in different
individuals.

The first appearance of Borges in *Performance* comes
when Rosebloom is seen sitting in a car reading Borges's
Ficciones, whiling away the time as Chas goes about his
business of putting the frighteners on a Cypriot blue-
movie exhibitor. An unusual choice of reading matter
for an East End hood, perhaps.

The next Borges reference surfaces in the first exchange
between Turner and Chas as they discuss the latter's
assumed occupation as a juggler.

> *Turner*: Cheops in his bloody pyramid, he dug a
> juggle or two, eh? Remember. And the Tetriarchs
> of Sodom and Orbis Tertius – they juggled their
> ancient black magical balls fit to bust and no mistake
> . . . Right? Am I right, baby?
> *Chas*: More or less. Personally, I just, you know . . .
> perform.

'Orbis Tertius' is the name of an encylopaedia that
describes the life and customs of the imaginary middle-
eastern country of Uqbar in Borges's story 'Tlon, Uqbar,
Orbis Tertius'.

This story moves from the discovery of an elusive
encyclopaedia article about Uqbar to the ultimate revelation of a 300-year-old conspiracy of idealist philosophers
and intellectuals, who have been plotting the invention of

a new and totally consistent planet, Tlon. Tlon's classic culture, we are told, consists of a single discipline – psychology. The planet's metaphysicians 'seek not truth or even the appearance of truth but amazement . . . One of Tlon's schools even denies time', reasoning that 'the present is ill-defined, the future has no reality other than as present hope, and the past has no reality other than as present memory. A second school claims that *all time* has already passed and that our lives are little more than the dim or doubtless falsified or twisted memory or reflection of a series of actions that cannot be recovered.' Yet another school maintains that 'while we are asleep here, elsewhere we are awake, so that each of us in fact is two people'.

The spectre of Borges surfaces again later in the film, in the kitchen in Powis Square, when Turner reads aloud Borges's story 'El Sur' ('The South') to Pherber and Lucy. 'The South' tells the story of Juan Dahlmann, a Buenos Aires librarian and the grandson of German Protestants, who dreams of one day retiring to the house he still owns on what had once been extensive family property. After an accident, in which he grazes his scalp on a freshly painted open casement window, Dahlmann is taken to hospital with blood poisoning. Racked with fever and nightmares, he hangs between life and death.

After his recovery, Dahlmann decides to convalesce at his small *estancia* out on the plains to the south of the province of Buenos Aires. '"Tomorrow I'll wake up at the ranch", he reflects, and it was almost as if at one and the same time he were two men – the man moving through that autumn day and the countryside of his native land,

and his double, confined to a hospital bed and subjected to endless observation.'

On the journey, Dahlmann is obliged to get off the train at a place he does not recognise. He dines at a humble inn, where he notices an old man huddled on the floor against the bar. 'Small, dark and leathery, he seemed to exist outside time, in an eternity.' Dahlmann sees in this gaucho a symbol of the South that he has made his own destiny. Moments later, some young hoodlums at another table pelt Dahlmann with pellets of bread, and soon one of them challenges him to a fight. The withered gaucho throws the unarmed Dahlmann a knife. 'It was as though the South had decided that Dahlmann accept the challenge.'

As they step outside, Dahlmann knows that he is lost, but 'while he felt no hope neither did he feel fear. Crossing the threshold, Dahlmann felt that to die in a knife fight under the open sky and on his feet would have been, that first night in the hospital, when they stuck him with the needle, a liberation, a happiness, a festivity. He felt that if he had been able then to choose or dream his own death, this is the death he would have chosen or dreamed.'

In the film, a similar recognition can be seen in Turner, who chooses a ritualistic and purifying death at the hands of Chas, rather than the slow psychic death his inertia portends.

The final act of homage to Borges occurs in the scene in which Chas shoots Turner. As the camera follows the trajectory of the bullet into Turner's cerebral cortex, the face of Borges suddenly appears – a benign priest, it seems, officiating over the merging of the two men.

Borges died of liver cancer in Switzerland in 1986. There is no record of him ever having seen *Performance*.

Breton, Michèle (b. 1951)

French actress whose performance as Lucy was to be her one and only film role.

For many years after the making of the film, Michèle Breton was to be the enigma at the heart of the *Performance* story. Those who had worked on the film, or known Breton for the short time that she was associated with Cammell's circle, could cast little light on where she had come from, or what had happened to her when filming was completed.

Sandy Lieberson remembers her as 'one of Donald's little girlfriends, someone he'd picked up in France who didn't care who she slept with. A strange little creature, totally androgynous-looking – the way Donald liked them.'

Myriam Gibril, who became Cammell's girlfriend after the making of *Performance* and knew Breton in London, remembers her as 'just a little girl who happened to be picked up at the right time in the right place for that purpose. She represented that image that Donald was so in love with – that young girl who is totally uninhibited, no hang-up whatsoever.'

By Cammell's own account he had met Breton in St Tropez. He had brought her to Paris and then to London to make *Performance*. It is clear from the early drafts of the script that Cammell already had her in mind to play the part of Lucy. Breton was just seventeen, and Cammell was obliged to falsify her age to secure the necessary work permits.

Breton was an erratic, and sometimes disturbing, presence throughout the filming. Cammell would later recall that she 'smoked too much' hash and was also frequently under the influence of psychedelics. She was peculiarly accident-prone. On at least two occasions, workmen had to be dispatched to her Knightsbridge flat to repair a bathroom window which she had smashed.

According to Cammell, while Breton was in London, she spent time with some French boys who were a 'malign influence'. After the film was completed she returned with them to Paris, where she had become heavily involved in drugs. 'It was very sad.'

Breton then appeared to vanish off the face of the earth. Anita Pallenberg heard she had been admitted to a sanatorium. Marianne Faithfull thought she had died – 'perhaps in Marseilles'.

In 1995, the author found Breton, living in Berlin. By her own account, she was born and grew up in a small town in Brittany, but had always hankered after excitement. 'I had my problems.' When she was sixteen, her parents gave her 100 francs, put her on a train to Paris and told her they never wanted to see her again.

She drifted to St Tropez, where she met Donald Cammell. 'He told me I was pretty.' Cammell took her with him to Paris, where she started modelling for fashion magazines and was drawn into the party scene, while living in a *ménage à trois* with Cammell and his girlfriend of the time, Deborah Dixon. 'Everybody was sleeping with everybody,' Breton remembered. 'It was those times.'

Her memories of making *Performance* were confused. She had never acted before, she said, and she was stoned all of the time. 'I was very young and very disturbed. I didn't know what I was doing and they used me. It was a very spaced-out atmosphere. There was no love there, no understanding between the people. Everybody was on a heavy ego-trip. James Fox was the only person who had some human communication. He saw what was going on with me – the emptiness. He understood that, and he was very gentle to me.

'James was always the outsider. He was playing the part of the outsider, and in real life it was like that too.'

After the film, she said, she felt 'used up'.

'I was taking everything that was going. I was in a very bad shape, all fucked up. Donald drove me to Paris. I went to his place and stayed for two or three days, and then he told me he didn't want to see me any more.' She had no money and a growing drug habit. For five years she drifted around France and Spain. On the island of Formentera she was busted for possession of drugs and returned to Paris, on the run from the police.

In Paris, a friend told her that drugs were cheap in Afghanistan, so she made her way to Kabul. She lived there for a year, shooting morphine, selling her passport, her belongings, everything. One night she took LSD. 'I looked at my needles, my drugs and said never again.'

From Kabul, she travelled to India, where she was hospitalised for three months. She returned to Kabul, then to Italy, and eventually to Berlin, where she has lived for the past thirteen years.

'I've done nothing with my life,' she said. 'Where did

it start going wrong? I can't remember. It's something like destiny.'

She last saw *Performance* in 1987. 'I was feeling kind of sick looking at this. It was a feeling of death.'

Burroughs, William (1914–97)

American beat author, whose novels such as *Junkie*, *The Naked Lunch* and *The Soft Machine* were among Donald Cammell's favourite reading matter. Burroughs's themes of sexual transgression, addiction, violence and mind-control made him a cult author and an influential figure on the nascent London underground in the mid-Sixties. Both Cammell and Roeg were particularly intrigued by Burroughs's 'cut-ups', a technique of chopping up texts and rearranging them in random order to subvert the power of 'the word', which Burroughs had developed with the surrealist Brion Gysin in Paris. Roeg was in the audience when *The Cut-Ups*, a film made by Burroughs and Anthony Balch, was shown in London in 1966, and the cut-ups philosophy can be seen as one of the influences which foreshadowed the radical editing techniques employed in *Performance*.

It's likely that Cammell first learned of the legend of the 'Old Man of the Mountain' through Burroughs. Burroughs and Gysin became obsessed with the legend during their stay in Paris, and Burroughs makes mention of it in his book *Exterminator!*.

In his early draft for *Performance*, entitled **The Performers**, Cammell makes a sly reference to Brion Gysin, when Lucy suggests that Chas should hide out in Marrakesh – 'He

could stay with Professor Gysin, couldn't he?' That scene
was dropped from the final script, but Burroughs himself
– *el hombre invisible* – surfaces in *Performance* in the scene
where Pherber bathes the wounds on Chas's back. 'Maybe
we ought to call Dr Burroughs,' she says. 'Give him a
shot . . .' Burroughs would surely have obliged.

C

Cammell, David (b. 1936)

Younger brother of Donald Cammell, and associate producer of *Performance*. At the time, David Cammell was a partner in the company Cammell-Hudson-Brownjohn, making television commercials. The Hudson of the partnership – Hugh – went on to enjoy success as the director of *Chariots of Fire* and sundry other films.

As associate producer, David Cammell was responsible for establishing locations, ensuring the film stayed on budget and 'trouble-shooting' day-to-day production problems.

In 1998, he acted as the executive-producer of *Final Performance*, a documentary film about Donald Cammell's life, directed by Chris Rodley and Kevin MacDonald.

Cammell, Donald (1934–96)

It is impossible to separate *Performance* from the life and times of its writer, co-director and the man whose ideas and philosophy the film embodies – Donald Cammell. Like Orson Welles and *Citizen Kane*, the film stands as the benchmark of his professional life, his memorial and epitaph.

Cammell was born on 17 January 1934 in Edinburgh, the first of three sons of Charles Richard Cammell and Iona Macdonald.

Charles Cammell was a scion of the ship-building family Cammell-Laird. As a young man, he led the life of a dilettante, living in a moated château in Burgundy, writing poetry and cultivating an interest in the arts. By the 1930s, his personal fortune had been lost in the financial crash and his marriage had ended. Cammell returned to Britain. In 1932 he married for the second time, and settled in the Outlook Tower, adjacent to Edinburgh Castle, where Donald was born.

The young Donald Cammell grew up in a fiercely bohemian atmosphere. His father was an associate editor of the art magazine the *Connoisseur* and joint proprietor of the *Atlantis Quarterly: A Journal Devoted to Atlantean and Occult Studies*. Donald would later recall that the household was 'filled with magicians, metaphysicians, spiritualists and demons'. Foremost among them was Aleister Crowley, the self-styled 'magus', pornographer and mountaineer, whom in the Twenties the British press would dub 'The Wickedest Man in the World'.

Charles Cammell met Crowley in 1936, when his worst years of notoriety were behind him; the two men became friends, and Cammell wrote an affectionate memoir: *Crowley, The Man, The Mage and the Magician*, which was published in 1951. (It was subsequently retitled *Aleister Crowley: The Black Magician*). Crowley would occasionally visit the Cammell home, and in later life Donald Cammell would enjoy regaling friends with the story of how as a young boy he had been bounced on the knee of 'the wickedest man in the world', and showing them the antique Chinese coin which Crowley had given him as a keepsake.

From an early age, Donald was a prodigiously gifted painter. At the age of eight his work was exhibited at the Royal Drawing Society. He was educated at Westminster public school, but at sixteen he won a scholarship to the Royal Academy. He went on to study in Florence with Annigoni, who was at that time the leading portrait painter in Europe, then returned to London, setting up as a portrait painter in his own studio in Flood Street, Chelsea.

Intelligent, gifted and debonair, Cammell was an immediate *succès d'estime*. In 1953 his painting of Sheridan, the Marquis of Dufferin and Ava, who was a pageboy at the coronation of the Queen, was acclaimed by *The Times* as 'society portrait of the year'. He married a Greek actress, Maria Andipa, who gave birth to a son, Amadis.

But the limitations of social portraiture – and the prospect of fatherhood – bored Cammell. His marriage disintegrated and he moved to New York, where he was to meet a stunningly beautiful fashion model named Deborah Dixon, with whom he was to spend the next ten years, and who subsequently worked as the costume designer on *Performance*.

In New York, Cammell's painting began to change. Influenced by Balthus, he concentrated more and more on nubile young women – a subject matter that enabled him to facilitate his sexual enthusiams, but which failed to satisfy him artistically. 'He was trying to find a style of painting that he felt happy with,' says David Cammell, 'but he never achieved that, and I don't think he was actually attuned to what was happening in modern art at the time. I think he felt, like a lot of other painters, that painting was pretty well dead.'

At the turn of the decade, Cammell and Dixon moved to Paris. Deborah was successful enough as a model to support them both, and Cammell turned his attention to film and literature.

Along with his brother David he wrote his first script in 1967 for a film called *The Touchables*, a modish thriller about a young rock star who is kidnapped by his friends. The script was passed over to Ian La Frenais, and the film vanished without trace. More germane to Cammell's future was *Duffy*, made in that same year, which Cammell co-scripted with Harry Joe Brown Jnr (Cammell's original script was entitled *Avec, Avec* – a gambling term). A 'caper movie', loosely based on the true story of an American jewel-thief named Albie Baker, and directed by Robert Parish, *Duffy* was an artistic failure, and a source of considerable frustration to Cammell, but it none the less had the effect of convincing him that the excitement, and his future, lay in film-making.

In his BFI monograph on *Performance*, Colin MacCabe makes the interesting point that, when Cammell submitted a list of his favourite films in the Nineties, almost none of them came from the period of the mid-to-late Sixties when Cammell was making the transition from painting to film, and most post-date *Performance*. Stanley Kubrick's *Dr Strangelove* (1963); Mike Leigh's *Naked* (1993); Jean-Luc Godard's *Nouvelle Vague* (1990); Murakami's *Tokyo Decadence Topaz* (1991); Ridley Scott's *Blade Runner* (1982); Bernardo Bertolucci's *The Conformist* (1969); Sergei Eisenstein's *Ivan the Terrible* (1942–6); Akira Kurosawa's *Throne of Blood* (1957) and Luis Buñuel's *The Discreet Charm of the Bourgeoisie* (1972). Cammell's greatest passions, it seems, were literature — notably the writing of Borges, Genet and Burroughs (all of whom were to prove hugely influential on *Performance*); theatre, and rock and roll — not least the Rolling Stones.

In Paris, Cammell had become friends with Anita Pallenberg and her boyfriend Brian Jones of the Stones (Pallenberg was a friend of Deborah Dixon). The dandified and narcissistic and self-absorbed figure of Jones made a powerful impression on Cammell (he would later describe Jones as 'an artefact') and it was through Jones that he was introduced to Mick Jagger and to the peculiar London circle made up of *louche* aristos, artists and musicians.

Cammell had a knack of making people fall in love with him. Erudite, witty and intellectually brilliant, he could talk knowledgeably about literature, film, physics and philosophy. 'He was an autodidact. He read voraciously. And he had a magnetic personality and he exploited it,' says his brother David. 'He was one of those people — once met, never forgotten. He was terribly attractive, charming, very intense. People really loved him.'

'It was amazing he wasn't gay,' says Chris Rodley, the film-maker and a friend. 'Intellectually, he was both sexes, in his head, if not in practice. He liked beautiful people. His fascination with Brian Jones was that Brian conducted his life like an artefact, and Donald did that. He was an aesthete. He was the kind of person who, if he said, come to hell with me, you'd say, OK; how bad can it be?'

Women, in particular, found Cammell irresistible, and his sexual enthusiasms were legendary. Myriam Gibril, who became Cammell's lover after the making of *Performance*, describes him as 'so charming it took me five years to realise he was shorter than I was'. He particularly liked threesomes. The *ménage à trois* that he created in *Performance* was modelled on his own experiences. At various times he had lived in *ménages à trois* with Anita Pallenberg, Michèle Breton and Deborah Dixon.

In late 1967, Cammell moved from Paris to London to begin work on *Performance*. It was to occupy the next year of his life. When filming was completed, he retreated to Spain with Myriam Gibril. Gibril was a strikingly beautiful French-Ethiopian model and actress, thirteen years younger than Cammell.

Warner, meanwhile, was deliberating over what to do with *Performance*. Executives were in despair over the rushes they had seen. In 1969, Cammell flew to California, where he spent the next year re-editing the film. He was to remain in Hollywood for the rest of his life.

'He liked the milieu,' says David Cammell. 'He liked the beautiful women, obviously. And he felt that was the powerhouse of film-making.'

Cammell rented a small wood and brick house on Crescent Drive, at the highest point in the Hollywood Hills, offering a panoramic view across the city, from the skyscrapers of downtown Los Angeles to the Pacific Ocean.

He set to work on a script called *Ishtar*, a story about a Supreme Court judge who gets kidnapped by bandits while on holiday in Morocco. Cammell wanted the beat writer William Burroughs to play the judge. But he was unable to secure the financing for the film. While *Performance* had been a cult hit, Cammell's disagreements with Warner had left an indelible mark.

'Donald was too clever for Hollywood,' says Chris

Rodley. 'People were intimidated by him. No-one likes to work with people who are too smart. Producers decode that as "movies full of references which no-one's going to get", which in Donald's case was also partly true.'

'When *Performance* eventually came out, a lot of producers came to Donald, but Donald wanted to pick and choose,' says Myriam Gibril. 'Producers as a rule are not the most refined people, and Donald was refined. His sensitivity got a little roughed up; and he was always hoping that somebody more *sympathique* would come along. It never happened. I can remember meetings with producers where they were saying, "How much money am I going to make?" It was always the bottom line. And that wasn't Donald's concern at all. People sell out every day of their life, they compromise. Donald wouldn't compromise.'

'The studios were afraid of Donald,' says Frank Mazzola, Cammell's editor on the final cut of *Performance* and on two later Cammell films. 'He didn't walk in on his knees looking for crumbs. He rubbed people up the wrong way. In Hollywood there's a certain protocol; as people move up the ladder they start stripping themselves of who they are, so they can be presentable to the guys with money, so the guys with money can feel safe. If somebody walks in that's different, it scares them.'

To the Hollywood establishment, Cammell was 'difficult', a bad risk. It was a stigma that would haunt him for the rest of his life.

From an early age, Donald Cammell had shown a tendency towards depression and a morbid preoccupation with death. According to his brother, David, Cammell

once told a friend that he had thought about killing himself
when he was seven years old. 'I suppose everybody does
that in a way,' says David. 'But I think even then it was
more serious with Donald. It was an intellectual process,
to do with control. You have the choice to go on living
or the choice to kill yourself.'

Among Cammell's friends was Kenneth Anger – the
underground film-maker and an authority on the life and
teachings of Aleister Crowley – who styled his own films
as 'magickal spells'. Anger persuaded Cammell to play
Osiris, the Egyptian god of death, in his 1970 film *Lucifer
Rising*. (Myriam Gibril played Isis, goddess of life.) 'It was
typecasting,' said Anger. 'Donald was in love with death,
and Myriam was a life-force that would balance out his
gloomy side.'

Frustrated by the difficulties in getting films made in
Hollywood, Cammell's depression deepened, to the point
where it became intolerable for Gibril. 'You can only
listen to someone say they want to kill themselves so
many times,' she remembers. 'You say, come on, let's
move on. But it was no, I have to kill myself. He used
to rant about it. He could be this charming Donald, then
all of a sudden sink into this dark, dark mood. We were
staying in New York and one day he told me he was going
to go to the roof of the building and jump. That was too
visual for me.

'I could no longer help him as a muse, as someone
to lead him out of his dark corner. And if you can no
longer do that then you have no place to be there. It's
your downfall. If you stay, you're going to drown.'

There was another reason why Cammell's relationship

with Gibril was foundering. Gibril was now almost thirty, and Cammell had always liked younger women.

'Donald came from an era when women were not your equal,' says Gibril. 'He reminded me of a book I read once where old Chinese men would pay young girls to sleep with them, almost to suck up the energy of youth. After years and years, that's the picture I had. By staying around young women he was in this no-man's-land of eternal youth. They don't ask questions, they don't challenge.'

In Los Angeles, Cammell had become friends with a fourteen-year-old girl named China Kong, the younger daughter of Marlon Brando's lover, Anita Kong. In his role of paterfamilias, Brando attempted to scare off Cammell, but the friendship held, and when China was eighteen she and Cammell married. They would remain together until Cammell's death.

China's original ambition was to be a painter, but under Cammell's tutelage she started collaborating with him on scripts. Often she would write the male parts and Cammell the female. 'Donald moulded her,' says David Cammell. 'He made her what she was.'

Cammell had more or less written his son from his first marriage out of his life, and the marriage to China would produce no children.

'Donald was very uncomfortable with the whole idea of children,' says Drew Hammond, a scriptwriter and a close friend of Cammell's in the last three years of his life. I knew him for quite a long time before he even admitted he had a son, and he seemed very uncomfortable with the whole idea of it. He hadn't had contact with him for many, many years, and was not the least bit interested in having contact, unfortunately.

'I think it went deeper than considering it a limitation on his freedom. If I had to guess, I would say that deep down, in many ways, while Donald valued himself as an artist and had great confidence in his abilities as an artist, he didn't feel that way about himself as a human being.'

Another friend puts it differently. 'China was his child.'

In his first twenty-five years in Hollywood, Cammell completed only two feature films. In 1977, he made *Demon Seed*, starring Julie Christie as a woman who is impregnated by a computer. Eleven years were to elapse until his next feature, *White of the Eye*, a study of a woman who is unknowingly married to a serial killer.

Both bore the unmistakable signature of Cammell, the almost hallucinatory narrative technique, the obsessions with sex and death, viewed with an unsparingly clinical detachment. Both were diluted and compromised by studio interference, leaving Cammell in despair.

In the years between, he survived on development deals, the occasional rock music video and writing scripts that would never get made: an adaptation of Nabokov's *Pale Fire*; a script about the relationship between Lady Hamilton and Nelson called *Pharaoh*; and a script called *Hot*, written for Mick Jagger.

His greatest frustrations, however, were caused by Marlon Brando. Cammell and Brando first met in Paris in the Sixties, over a hospital bed. (Brando, bizarrely, was recuperating from an accident where he had spilt scalding coffee on his testicles.) Cammell was enormously impressed

by the actor, and an early treatment of *Performance* was actually written with Brando in mind. (see **The Performers**).

Brando, for his part, was apparently impressed both by
Performance and *Demon Seed* and in 1978, the altercation
over China apparently forgotten, he invited Cammell to
collaborate on a project called *Fan Tan*, a story about an
adventurer travelling in the South Seas who falls in love
with a woman pirate. Cammell collaborated on a script,
but the project was scrapped when Brando lost interest.

Brando then suggested that Cammell should write a
novel based on the film treatment. Again, he set to
work, completing half the manuscript before Brando,
again, aborted the project.

In 1989, Brando approached Cammell for a third time,
with a view to directing a script which Brando was writing
– a CIA thriller called *Jericho*. Cammell spent eighteen
months preparing the film and it went as far as pre-
production in Mexico when Brando again pulled out.

For all his frustration with Hollywood, however, Cammell
never thought of leaving. 'I think he recognised that
Hollywood, despite all its faults, was the centre of the film
universe,' says Drew Hammond. 'He would have regarded
going to Europe as a backward step. Even though he never
claimed to be a resident here. He lived in California for
twenty-five years, but he always said, "I'm a resident of
France."'

But he was always to one side of the film community.
His friends tended to be writers, scientists, intellectuals –
not actors or agents. 'He was not a buddy-buddy person,'
says Myriam Gibril. 'You had to earn his respect.' In his
later years, he saw fewer and fewer people, venturing

out only occasionally, usually with China to a local Thai restaurant, notable for its particularly pretty waitresses.

In 1994, Cammell started work on what was to be his last film, *Wild Side*, a thriller written by him and China about the relationship between a prostitute and a money-launderer.

NuImage, which produced the film, was a company that specialised in low-budget violence and sexploitation movies for the video and cable-TV markets. Cammell, they hoped, would add artistic legitimacy to their name. For his part, Cammell could no longer afford to be choosy. But the shoot was fraught with problems over the budget and NuImage refused to accept Cammell's first cut, replete with his trademark flashbacks, instead re-editing the film in a more straightforward way to emphasise its sexual content. Cammell responded by executing his own cut on Avid, with a view to sorting out a distribution deal of his own. But in the meantime, NuImage sold its cannibalised cut to cable TV. Cammell took his name off the film. NuImage prevented him using the standard Hollywood pseudonym, Alan Smithee. Instead the film was credited to Franklin Browner.

'It was a terrible embarrassment for him, because they turned it into an exploitation movie,' says David Cammell. 'He was personally involved with the artists, and he felt he'd let them down.'

Cammell was downcast by the farrago, but worse was to come. During the making of *Wild Side*, China had begun an affair with a younger man who had been working on the film. At the conclusion of the film, she left Crescent Drive. Cammell was devastated.

By now, his manic-depressive tendencies had begun to take a rather idiosyncratic form. According to Drew Hammond, Cammell suffered from a form of dissociated personality order. 'He would practically become another person whom he would call "the uncensored Don",' remembers Hammond. 'That person was somebody who was very much the opposite of Donald's ordinary persona, in the sense that he was extremely outgoing, spontaneous, he would do all kinds of crazy things – like get up in the middle of a movie theatre and start doing a little performance, or he would sing opera in Italian.'

On one occasion, the 'uncensored Don' jumped into his car, naked, and sped off into the night. He was stopped by the police, doing 100mph down a freeway, but managed to talk his way out of it.

'It was always my view that this condition grew out of his love for China,' says Hammond. 'It was very entertaining for her. But in the end, when he was terribly depressed over the state of *Wild Side*, the uncensored Don, instead of appealing to China, began to become disconcerting to her.

'The reason she gave for leaving was that it became too difficult to endure Donald being depressed and the uncensored Don saying nasty things. And that made him much more depressed – more depressed than China realised. She was everything to Donald.

'Everything he did had more to do with his aims for the relationship with China than its apparent objective, and that included film-making. She was the most important thing in his life – in that way he was a very romantic figure.'

Cammell had always had a passion for guns. For years he kept a 9mm Glock pistol, which he would sometimes carry to meetings with producers, tucked in his pocket, almost as a talisman. According to Hammond, the 'uncensored Don' would sometimes hide the pistol, and go for weeks without being able to find it. 'But when he was in a depressed state he would keep it with him, like a security-blanket.'

'I went across to see him and I was terribly disturbed by him,' says David Cammell. 'He was certainly talking about suicide. I stayed with him for six weeks, but by the time I left I was quite confident he was OK.'

Drew Hammond was so concerned about his friend's deepening depression that he persuaded him to see a doctor. David Cammell had already tried the same tack. For a while, Cammell took anti-depressants, but he said they only made him feel worse.

The débâcle over *Wild Side* had left Cammell in a parlous state. He was so broke that at one stage he considered selling his collection of stills from *Performance* to tide him over.

'The last time I saw him, he was in a desperate situation,' says Frank Mazzola. 'Films weren't coming together; he'd run out of money. But he was like a kid. You know when you're twelve or thirteen and you want to hang out with your buddies in the playground? He was like that.

'Ever since *Performance*, he and I had been talking about forming an independent production company, getting away from the studios because when he was at Warner Bros he was going nuts. That night, for some reason, he started talking about it again. We went out to dinner, and he was saying, "We're going to do our stuff." There was such a sense of hope and innocence about him. It was almost like there was an angelic sense to him at the end.'

Suddenly, Cammell's fortunes seemed to change. By early 1996, China's affair with the younger man had apparently burned out, and she returned to the house on Crescent Drive. Cammell was working on a new script with Drew Hammond called *33*, about the birth of the heroin trade, set in Istanbul and Marseilles, and China joined them as a collaborator.

The film was, by general consensus, Cammell's best script in years.

'He called me up and said, "I don't get it – everyone loves the script. What have I done wrong?",' says Chris Rodley. 'He did interpret that quite seriously that he'd done something wrong. Everyone likes it; everyone likes the people. He never wanted anything to be easy in that way. Any optimism was a no-no. It was all hard wired.

'He had a strange reaction to good news; it would often send him into a terrible depression. It was that thing of, when you're up, the only way is down. You don't want that fall, and you will get it. He obviously thought he'd written a commercial, likeable script, and it worried the shit out of him.'

On 22 April, Cammell received a telephone call from his agents, telling him that Bill Pullman, the Hollywood star, had provisionally agreed to take the lead role – a virtual guarantee that money could be raised to make the film.

The next day, China Cammell was working in the study of Crescent Drive when Donald walked into the room and placed some papers on her desk. Among them was a letter, absolving her of any responsibility for what he was about to do. He then walked into the bedroom, picked up his pistol and shot himself in the head.

Cammell knew something of ballistics. He certainly would have known that the surest way to kill himself would have been by directing the gun upwards through the mouth. But he directed the shot at the top of his head – the same shot that kills Turner in *Performance*. It allegedly took Donald Cammell some forty minutes to die. China subsequently told friends that in that time her husband appeared happy, almost euphoric. He is said to have asked her to hold up a mirror, so that he could see his face. He is also said to have asked her, 'Do you see the picture of Borges?'

According to Drew Hammond, Cammell had often talked about suicide. 'Donald believed that he would be annihilated on his death; that his soul would not survive. He thought there was nothing immoral about killing yourself.

'The idea of suicide was something very ingrained in him, that he had thought about for many years. He always assumed that's the way he would die. I think it's the way he wanted it.'

'In the end I think it was a positive thing for Donald,' says Chris Rodley. 'He wanted the experience of what it was like to die – he'd always wanted the experience – and he got it – forty minutes of it. It's all there in *Performance*. I don't think it's at all far-fetched to suggest that *Performance* was a kind of rehearsal. Because he'd read up so much about guns and so on, he knew exactly what he was doing. I think that was absolutely intentional. I think it was stage-managed; the last performance.'

Crowley, Aleister (1875–1947)

One of the more intriguing myths which has grown up around *Performance* concerns Donald Cammell's childhood association with Aleister Crowley, self-styled 'Magickian', and the man whom the British press honoured with the soubriquet 'the Wickedest Man in the World'.

Edward Alick Crowley (he later changed his name to Aleister) was born on 12 October 1875.

Crowley's parents were members of a fundamentalist Christian sect, the Plymouth Brethren, against whose moral strictures the young Crowley duly rebelled as soon as he was able. His religious upbringing made him vividly interested in the Biblical Satan and the Whore of Babylon from the Book of Revelations, and from the age of fifteen, when he was seduced by an actress in Torquay, he became an apostle of sexual freedom. His distraught mother fixed on her wayward son the name of 'the Beast', the man-monster of the Apocalypse whose number is 666. It gave him something to live up to.

Crowley was educated at Trinity College, Cambridge (his subject was Moral Science). A substantial inheritance removed the necessity of following a profession, allowing him to spend his life pursuing his three abiding interests – climbing, poetry and 'magick', as Crowley himself styled it. An expert mountaineer, he climbed throughout Europe, South America and Asia, and made an unsuccessful attempt on K2 in the Himalayas, the second highest mountain in the world. He published hundreds of poems and some fifty volumes on magick and related subjects. But it was as an occultist that Crowley was to gain his greatest notoriety.

In his early twenties he became an initiate of the Hermetic Order of the Golden Dawn, which included W.B. Yeats and Maude Gonne among its number (Yeats described Crowley as an 'unspeakable mad person'), but his wayward nature and his sense of his own manifest destiny was too large to be accommodated in any cabal but his own.

The turning point came over three days in 1904, in Cairo, when Crowley composed his most famous (or perhaps infamous) book, *The Book of the Law*, which he claimed was dictated to him by the 'direct voice' of his 'Guardian Angel' Aiwass – 'a messenger from the forces ruling this earth at present'. Its philosophy is best summarised by the phrase that Crowley adopted as his leitmotif, 'Do what thou wilt shall be the whole of the law.' Using *The Book of the Law* as revealed prophecy, Crowley declared himself the high priest of a new religion, Crowleyism, which he predicted would survive after the fall of Christianity.

He retreated to a manse on the shores of Loch Ness, 'Boleskine', where he busied himself by conjuring spirits, dabbling as a publisher and putting the fear of God, or the Devil, into the locals. Crowley enjoyed controversy and played up to his demonic image, styling himself variously as Count Vladimir Svareff, Count Swanoff and the Laird of Boleskine and Abertarff, dressing in robes and drenching himself in musk, which he claimed women found irresistible.

The phrase 'Do what thou wilt' is also to be found in Rabelais. It was the motto of the satirist's fabled institution, the Abbaye de Thélème, in which Rabelais parodied the rules and austerities of a religious community, imagining instead a cloistered retreat of unfettered freedoms and pleasures.

In 1920, Crowley and a motley bunch of acolytes and disciples retreated to Cefalù in Sicily, where he founded his own 'Abbey of Thelema' in a deserted villa. Crowley decorated the walls with sexually explicit murals and magical scenes, dominated by a fifteen-foot-high painting of Aiwass, and installed a shrine where small animals would occasionally be sacrificed.

To raise money for the enterprise, Crowley hastily wrote a book, *Confessions of a Drug Fiend*, a thinly veiled account of his own experiences with heroin and cocaine (Crowley had been prescribed heroin as a medicinal treatment for chronic bronchitis, and remained an addict until his death). Inevitably the book became a *cause du scandale*, alerting the British papers to his activities in Cefalù.

When an Oxford student died of typhus after drinking water from a polluted stream, the *Sunday Express* launched a campaign of vilification against Crowley, reporting that 'Children under ten, whom the Beast keeps at the "abbey" are made to witness horrible sexual debauches unbelievably revolting. Filthy incense is burned and cakes made of goats' blood and honey are consumed in the windowless room where the Beast conducts his rites. The rest of the time he lies in a room hung with obscene pictures collected all over the world, saturating himself with drugs.' Purple, certainly, but not, perhaps, wholly inaccurate. The periodical *John Bull* joined in with the campaign, anointing Crowley with the moniker that would haunt him for the rest of his days: 'The Wickedest Man in the World'.

The witch-hunt was taken up by newspapers in America and Europe, and in 1923 Crowley was expelled from Italy, a victim of Mussolini's purge against secret societies. He lived for a while in Paris, and then returned to London, broke and debilitated by ill-health with only his notoriety to sustain him.

It was at this point that he became friends with C.J. Cammell. Crowley lived near the Cammells in Richmond, Surrey and often came to call. Kenneth Anger, an authority on the life and work of Crowley, suggests that the visits were 'probably to cadge a meal' – Crowley never picked up a restaurant bill or repaid a loan in his life – although Cammell obviously had a profound respect and affection for the old magus, while disapproving of his 'magickal' ambitions.

Anger has even gone so far as to suggest that Donald Cammell was Crowley's 'magickal son', although Cammell never claimed as much himself publicly, and appeared to take an ambivalent view of Crowley.

According to David Cammell, 'Donald was interested in [Crowley] in a peripheral sort of way, just as a great character; but he wasn't remotely like him. Donald was a tremendous realist. He wasn't a mystic; he wasn't religious in any sense. He thought it was all a load of tosh.'

Intriguingly, however, Myriam Gibril, who was Cammell's girlfriend between 1969 and 1975, says that the subject of Crowley was 'taboo' between them. 'He wouldn't talk about it. Approach esotericism or those sort of subjects and Donald would say, darling can we talk about this tomorrow? Very softly, very nicely. But total avoidance.'

Christopher Isherwood once observed that 'The truly awful thing about Crowley is that one suspects he didn't really believe in anything. Even his wickedness. Perhaps the only thing that wasn't fake was his addiction to heroin and cocaine.'

Crowley died, poverty-stricken, in a nursing home in Hastings in 1947. According to the nurse who was at his bedside, his last words were 'Sometimes I hate myself.'

Cuthbertson, Allan (1920–88)

Australian-born character actor who played the role of Harley-Brown, the barrister who is intimidated by Chas, Moody and Rosebloom in the first half of the film.

Cuthbertson was regularly seen on British cinema and television screens through the Sixties and Seventies, most often in the role of snooty civil servants, army officers or aristocrats.

D

Dana

Night-club singer and girlfriend of Chas, with whom he is seen having sex in the film's opening scenes. The fashion model Vicki Hodge (who was then the girlfriend of John Bindon) was originally cast in the role of Dana, until Equity, the actors' union, intervened. The part instead went to a professional actress, the former Miss World Ann Sidney.

Dean, James (1931–55)

Iconic Fifties movie star, too fast to live, too young to die, whose picture can be glimpsed on the wall of Noel's/Chas's room in the basement of Powis Square. The probable inspiration for Cammell's choice of Chas's pseudonym, Johnny Dean.

Devlin, Chas

Enforcer for Harry Flowers, a man who takes pleasure in his work of violence and intimidation. A true professional. Or, as Flowers himself puts it, 'He's a nut-case like all artists. But I can rely on him. I can't say more than that, can I?'

In his preparatory text for *Performance*, entitled *The*

Performers, Donald Cammell offered a vivid picture of the character he had in mind for Chas:

> The role of a 'Front Man' is only to be found in the most sophisticated strata of crime; the criminal organisation. The Firm. To fill the role, it is not enough simply to be a giant thug (he will usually be accompanied by a bodyguard or two who admirably fulfill this role). A big firm (as opposed to a gang of casual tearaways) depends like its counterpart in the Upperworld upon its stock of goodwill (badwill?). To maintain this stock, respect — fearful respect — and, ideally, admiration (however qualified) must be maintained by Representatives of talent and ability. The man in charge of this department, working 'in the field' has executive status.
>
> To do his job perfectly, he need never use violence (though he must be capable of awesome violence, and be known to be capable of it — be known, ideally, to like it.) He must, rather, physically and psychically, incarnate violence. Inevitably a certain glamour is involved. (He is a 'Performer' in the dramatic as well as the villains' sense of the word.) He must be a symbolic vessel, containing and projecting an aura of threat, of imminent violence that, if he is good, need never actually materialise.

The character of Chas, Cammell continues, should be 'elegant, laconic, rarely smiling. Usually polite, if contemptuous. Sometimes bleakly funny. Occasionally threatening. Always menacing.'

*   *   *

What do we know of Chas Devlin's background? His
mother is Irish, but we can assume he was born in London,
although whether in the East End or that unmappable jun-
gle south of the river – Peckham, New Cross, Lewisham
or Catford – it's hard to tell. We surmise that he boxed as
a teenager (amateur, certainly, but was he a failed pro? Or
perhaps earning a living in illegal bouts?). A likely lad, hard
but clever. Perhaps he's served time in reform school or
borstal. Somewhere along the line he has come under the
care and influence of Harry Flowers, rising to the position
of his chief enforcer.

On the face of it, Chas is your straight-up-and-down thug:
a walking repository of the most reactionary working–class
values ('I'm a bit old-fashioned . . .'): sexist, xenophobic –
'You stink . . .' he tells the Cypriot owner of a blue-movie
club. 'Stinking foreign parasite' – hostile to anything
outside his own immediate experience; a man who turns
a face of pure, undiluted violence to the world. Only as the
film unfolds do we discern a more complex psychology.

For Cammell, Chas is important not only as a study in
public violence, but in also in its relationship to private
sexuality. His 'performance' is not simply a 'method act'
of controlled threat and intimidation; it is a paradigm
of a particular set of working–class perceptions about
what constitutes a man. And in breaking down his 'performance', Turner and Pherber are not only exploring
the roots of the violence from which Chas derives his
energy and sense of purpose – the violence that Turner
has lost and wants to recover; they are also dismantling Chas's view of his own masculinity, blurring the

borderline between male and female, homo- and hetero-
sexual.

In the opening moments of the film, Cammell studi-
ously establishes that, for Chas, the line between sex and
violence is indivisible. We see him having sex with his
girlfriend, the night-club singer Dana (this is too solipsistic,
too laden with implicit violence to be described as making
love). The camera dwells lovingly on Fox's pumped-
up torso. The following morning we find him dressing
for 'work', slapping on aftershave, opening a drawer
to reveal a carefully folded selection of under-shorts,
buttoning himself into a crisp white shirt, suit and tie.
The fastidious tidiness of his Scandinavian-style, swinging
bachelor surroundings (notice him fussily emptying the
ashtray of Dana's cigarette ends, aligning the magazines
and the *Playboy* folder on the coffee-table); the controlled
efficiency of his actions, all suggest a man whose nature is
wound as tightly as a clock. A pressure cooker.

(An echo of this fleeting collage of images can be found
in Paul Schrader's *American Gigolo*, where Richard Gere
as the young hustler is seen methodically choosing his
wardrobe for the evening's assignation, like an assassin
selecting his weapons.)

But Cammell leaves us in no doubt that behind this
façade of self-assured masculinity, lie repressed homosexual
inclinations.

His early script for *The Performers* makes quite blatant
allusions to Chas's sexual history, which were subsequently
excised from the film. After shooting Joey Maddocks, Chas
goes on the run. From a telephone-box in Wandsworth
he calls, first, Harry Flowers and then his friend Tony,

looking for help. When it is obvious that this will not be forthcoming, he makes a third telephone call to an old acquaintance, Dominic, described in the script as 'an old queen'. The suggestion is that there has been some sort of relationship between Dominic and Chas in the past, but on this occasion Dominic refuses Chas's plea for help.

> *Dominic*: I'm not, ah, alone. Why don't you call me tomorrow?
> (*Replacing the receiver, he lights a cigarette, leans back in his Louis XVI bed. He is, of course, quite alone.*)

In a subsequent version of the script, Dominic becomes 'Howard', an art-collector in Eaton Square. He takes the call from Chas reclining in a four-poster bed.

> What a nice surprise, Charles! ... Yes ... we must. We must do Venice together one day ... (*very ironic*) ... How sweet to accept my invitation, finally. Albeit at 5am – and almost two years after it was extended ...'

Again, Howard makes an excuse that he is unable to help Chas, that he has someone with him: '*Howard subsides onto his pillow. He is quite alone in his bed.*'

Howard/Dominic was dropped from the final version of the film.

The needle that exists between Chas and Joey Maddocks is, as Harry Flowers puts it 'double personal' – were they once lovers as well as rivals? The wrecking of Chas's flat

by Maddocks and his cronies makes an explicit accusation, a single word daubed on the wall in red paint – 'poof' – reinforced by the admission that Maddocks attempts to beat out of Chas by flaying him with a dog lead – 'SAY IT!' (In the first cut of the film, Maddocks goes further, goading Chas as he beats him: 'I bet you love that. You little twerp . . . you vicious little twerp . . . You always was a dirty little boy . . . A nasty perverted little boy . . . Say it . . . I want you to say "I am a little poof", eh? . . . Say it.' These lines were cut at Warner Bros' insistence.)

When Chas appears to faint, one of Maddocks's men urges him to 'Give him the kiss of life, Joey,' and Maddocks explodes in anger.

As Maddocks whips Chas, scenes of his sado-masochistic love-making with Dana (he whips her, she scars his back with her fingernails) flash on the screen, reinforcing for the viewer the association in Chas's mind between sex and violence. The expression on his face as he administers the *coup de grâce* to Maddocks – 'I am a bullet . . .' – is almost sensual in its pleasure.

Up until this point in the film, Chas has been a man totally in his own element. But as he steps across the threshold of Powis Square, everything changes.

In his treatment for *The Performers*, Cammell draws a vivid picture of Chas's state of mind as he infiltrates himself into Turner's *ménage*.

> Chas's situation is simple. He is a hunted animal.
> He has gone to earth in a ridiculous and, to him,
> despicable burrow; but for his purposes it is perfect.
> Every instinct and insight of his agile brain into the

workings of intellects among the Firm, and (though he fears them less) the Police, tell him that this house is, of all unlikely hideouts, the very last that the hunters would suspect.

'. . . A bunch of beatniks . . .' The run-down pad of a weird, dropped-out hippie . . . a seedy bower of faded flower-children . . . to the Law and to the Firm (obverse and reverse of the same Authority, created and supported by established order . . . the defined forces of violence and violent anti-violence, both parts of the comprehensive and established Universe) . . . to the World and to the Underworld. no 31 Melbury Terrace [Cammell's original location of Turner's home] and its occupants are outside the established order of things; a hole in the woodwork as alien as a lunar crater.

Here Chas is forced into a confrontation with all the elements which make up his 'performance', not only the violence implicit in his character, but his own sexuality.

It is Pherber who first challenges Chas on his fixed idea of his own masculinity. Lying on the bed in the aftermath of his drug experience, Chas preens as she runs her hands over his body, then recoils when she holds up the mirror to show his face reflected above her breast.

Pherber: You never feel female, hmmm?
Chas: No, never. I feel like a man.
Pherber: That's too bad. That's what's wrong with you, isn't it?
Chas: What do you mean?

Pherber: It's a man's, man's, man's world.
Chas: There's nothing wrong with me. I'm normal.

Pherber and Chas do not make love, but their encounter makes possible his subsequent relationship with Lucy – a figure who embodies everything to which he would previously have been hostile: androgynous sexuality, foreignness, otherness.

Freed from the prison of his own rigid masculinity, he is able to respond to her not as a sex-object, to be used and discarded as Dana was, but as an equal. There is a sense of something akin to wonder at the transformation he has undergone as he caresses her. 'You're a skinny little frog, aren't you . . . small titties, haven't you, you're like a small boy, that's what you're like . . . Like a little slim boy.' Even the simple gesture of fetching shampoo seems symbolic, a small act of kindness which would have been unimaginable earlier, and which, here, leads him upstairs to Rosebloom, and thus to his death.

In his script *The Performers*, Cammell describes this transformation as a form not simply of sexual catharsis but of spiritual awakening.

Lying on the bed with Lucy after making love, 'something in Chas has changed', Cammell writes. 'Perhaps, though, his screwed-up ego would refuse to face the fact that for a little while anyway, he is not trying to demonstrate that he is "nothing but a man". Perhaps he has realised that these three people are not concerned with the demonic and pathetic problems of gender that rot the human race . . . that they don't waste their lives and loves trying to define their sexes. Relived [sic] of this duty he is marvellously at ease. Lucy is happy too. She says things to him in French. He understands perfectly.'

Thus is Chas redeemed.

Donald Cammell: 'For me it was important that Chas created a presence of tremendous courage; a guy way into a land that he didn't know how to explore, ready to go toe to toe with his own destiny. These ideas moved me in Borges – people who were prepared to go out and meet their fate in a very adventurous way. His performance was the one that counts.'

Did They, or Didn't They? A Question of Penetration

One of the many pioneering aspects of *Performance* is the realism and intimacy of the scenes of love-making between Jagger, Pallenberg and Breton. The mood of the scene – an idyllic, lustrous paean to bisexuality, almost innocent in its sensuality – offers a stark counterpoint to the animalistic violence of Chas's seduction of Dana, a didactic illustration of the healthy and uninhibited sexuality of 'hippie' society versus the unhealthy repressions of the 'straight' world.

There are numerous accounts of just how close Jagger and Pallenberg became during the making of the film – arousing the ire of Pallenberg's boyfriend, Keith Richard, in the process – and part of the abiding, and more prurient, mythology of *Performance* is that the consummation of the relationship was caught for posterity by Nic Roeg, filming under the sheets with a 16mm camera while Cammell 'directed' the action from the other side of the bed.

In his book *Mick Jagger*, published in 1974, the American author Anthony Scaduto suggests that the love-making between Jagger and Pallenberg seen in the film is totally authentic. 'Marianne [Faithfull], who visited the set once and who knew there had been a scene in which Jagger makes love to both Anita and the young French girl and actually fucked them – the scene was cut from the final version of the film – told one friend: "I didn't say anything about Mick fucking Anita at the time of the film because I knew the only way for it to work was for him to really appeal to her. He was Brian and Keith in one, and that's the only time he hit with her. Because he was a combination of the two men she cared about."'

In her own autobiography, published more than twenty years later, Faithfull offered a revised perspective on the relationship between Jagger and Pallenberg: 'While the film was being made, I felt, quite erroneously, that I had nothing to worry about,' she wrote. 'I never imagined Mick would be sleeping with Anita.

'I see Anita as very much the victim of all this, the vulnerable one who should have been looked after and protected. Her break-up with Brian Jones during the previous year had been devastating. She already had a hard time distinguishing between what was real and what was imaginary, so it was only natural that she would find Mick's incarnation of Turner irresistible. Their characters were propelled towards each other, and since the membrane between life and fiction was so thin in the film, there was little to prevent it actually coming about.'

★   ★   ★

David Cammell, however, remains adamant that whatever happened off-camera, 'nothing happened under the bed-sheets'.

If you look at the out-takes from that scene all you see is a few panning shots of Mick's cock. Anita had a 16-mil camera and Nic had another one. In some of the out-takes you can see Donald under the sheets himself, directing the scene.

Humphries, the lab who printed the film, refused to print that scene. The day after the shooting, the clapper loader was making up the rushes, and he came to see me in the office to say, by the way, put a note on the camera-sheets, 'make sure that Mrs Bloggins doesn't view them tomorrow morning at the labs', because there were a few viewers, one of them was a woman, and it might be a bit iffy if she doesn't understand.

So I wrote a note in big letters and underlined it. And the next morning I got a phone call from the managing director saying, 'Mr Cammell, we've got a problem . . .' Inevitably, the rushes had been viewed by Mrs Bloggins, who had immediately gone racing upstairs to complain. The manager said, we cannot release these frames because we'll be open to prosecution under the Obscene Publications Act.

Sandy [Lieberson] and I went over, and there was the chairman and the managing-director of Humphries; they had the rushes on the desk and next to them was a hammer and chisel. He passed across one set of tins, which was the negative, and

then picked up the other set, which contained the
print itself. He opened it up and set about the print
with the hammer and chisel in front of our eyes.
He then said, 'Don't leave by the front door, Mr
Cammell, and don't tell anybody I've done this.'
And he passed over the negatives.

I called Technicolor and explained the problem
and they just ran off the prints. I took the whole
picture away from Humphries – they lost the lot.

Some of the out-takes from that scene were later shown
at the **Wet Dream Festival** in Amsterdam.

'I always thought that the footage had been sneaked out
of the back-door at Technicolor,' says David Cammell.
'But to my amazement it was Sandy Lieberson who had
got hold of it and given it to the festival organisers.'

Drugs

Before *Performance*, Hollywood's limited flirtation with
the psychedelic experience had largely been confined to
the cinematic shorthand of a kaleidoscopic lens, a paisley
wardrobe and the obligatory soundtrack of sitar music –
drugs as social aberration, novelty or sensationalism.

Performance, uniquely, addressed the Sixties drug culture
on its own terms: a film about drugs made by people for
whom drugs were a part of everyday life. More than that,
it was the first film properly to examine the use of drugs
as an assault on the values of 'straight' society, and as an
instrument of personal transformation and change.

In *Performance* the drugs of choice are hashish and

psychedelics – reflecting the communal bonding of the shared joint, or the brave, solitary psychedelic journey of self-exploration. There is the only slightest, teasing reference to heroin, which had recently begun to infiltrate the Stones' circle (see **Vitamin B12**), and no mention at all of cocaine, which, within a few years, would be ubiquitous in rock music circles.

The aroma of hashish pervades *Performance* (as it is said to have pervaded the set throughout the shooting of the film), not as an exotic curiosity but as an habitual element of the daily domestic round.

The mood of Turner's *ménage* is set early on in the film when Pherber is seen rolling a joint while Turner lounges in the bath and Lucy rambles in a semi-coherent fashion about her problems with immigration.

Kick-starting the day with a five-skinner and a bath with two naked girls has never seemed so domestically routine. This, after all, is how rock stars lived – or at least were supposed to live. In the charmed circle of Jagger, Pallenberg, Cammell et al. it was possibly how everyone lived.

Joints are lit, smoked and passed at regular intervals thereafter, the hip relaxant/intoxicant of choice (note Turner's palpable expression of distaste when Chas asks if there's any Scotch – the 'straight' world's drug – in the house).

Jagger had taken his first acid trip a year earlier, at the famous Redlands weekend (see **Mars Bars**), and LSD was common currency in the circle. But it is not acid that Turner and Pherber use to dismantle Chas's 'performance' and see what makes him tick, but a fly agaric mushroom.

*   *   *

Our first sight of mushrooms is in a growing-box, placed incongruously outside the front door of 81 Powis Square, when Chas first arrives. Later, Pherber gathers a fly agaric from the garden, and serves it to Chas as she and Turner prepare him for the passport-photo. Chas, of course, has no idea that the mushroom is psychedelic.

> *Pherber*: Oh, you like them fried.
> *Chas*: Yes, I prefer them fried.
> *Pherber*: Would you like to try this?
> *Chas*: Yeah. I'll try anything once.
> *Pherber*: Yes. Have a taste.
> *Chas*: Yeah. you're a good cook, Pherber.

The fly agaric (*Amanita muscaria*) grows commonly through-out the British isles. It can vary in size from barely an inch tall to specimens a foot tall and almost a foot across, which look more like small tables. Accounts of the use of fly agaric occur in the practices of Siberian shamans. And Gordon Wasson, the mycologist and an early researcher into psychedelics, believed that the fly agaric was Soma, the drink described in the Rig-Veda which awakens man to his own divinity, and which, itself, was worshipped as a god.

The effects of fly agaric can be highly variable, depend-ing on the dose and the state of mind of the user, invoking feelings either of intense ecstasy and illumination, or of acute paranoia and mental unease. In Chas's case, both effects come into play.

In his study of the myths and rituals of psychedelic

mushrooms, *Strange Fruit*, Clark Heinrich notes that among experienced users in Siberia, 'three dried caps' is considered the average effective dose, although for a novice this would be considerably too much. He cautions that the 'age and weight' of the consumer should also be taken into account, adding that 'any experimentation should be done in safe, protected surroundings with a sitter who is not intoxicated'.

Turner: How much did you give him?
Pherber: Two thirds of the big one.
Turner: It's insane. I can't make it . . .'
Pherber: Well, you should have thought of that before . . .'

Heinrich tells us that the experience follows a customary path. Nausea in varying degrees is commonly experienced in the early stages, along with acute visual distortion. But once the nausea has passed, Heinrich notes, 'things to start to look up'. Sometimes a tremendous vitality is felt, as if one could conquer the world. Along with this comes a powerful urge to speak of the 'godliness and wonderful power' the user is experiencing. 'In this state one feels incapable of saying anything that is not true.' There may be feelings of intense euphoria and bliss. After a certain threshold has been crossed, thoughts are 'reduced' and the mind 'becomes like a clear pool in which no ripple stirs the surface' – a state which Heinrich compares to the yogic state of *samadhi*, or unity with the Divine.

Heinrich also describes, from his own experience, the possible negative effects of ingesting fly agaric. 'Existence was black, and blackness was all that existed. Darkness was on the face of the deep, assuming it had a face; it was too dark to tell. In the midst of this unknowing, this no-thing, a point of awareness arose, and it floated there forever. I no longer existed. There was only a feeble awareness adrift in the yawning maw of the void.'

Chas runs the entire gamut of these feelings. At first, he is entranced by the flickering light of a candle – 'I've never seen that sort before. They must be scorching hot' – and by the shimmering beauty of a mosaic table, which he immediately wants to buy: 'How much do you want for this table, Turner?'

As the drug takes hold, his assumed identity as 'Johnny Dean', night-club juggler, begins to evaporate in a hallucinogenic haze. Chas admires himself in a mirror and calls out for Rosebloom. 'Come on . . . we got to shift on . . . We're going to nudge that slag, don't worry about that . . .' When Pherber holds up a mushroom for Chas to inspect he recoils in horror. 'Horrible looking thing . . .' When she tells him he has eaten one he accuses her of poisoning him. 'No, no, no . . .' Pherber says, 'I just wanted to speed things up . . . I want to get a shift on.'

Disorientated, out of control, Chas falls into the bath screaming. Pherber takes his gun.

'I just want to go in there, Chas,' Turner tells him. 'This blood of this vegetable . . . is boring a hole.

'The second hole. It's penetrating the hole of your face, the skull of the bone . . . I just want to get right in there . . . you know what I mean? And root around like a Mandragora and grab and pull out something I need . . .' (The Mandragora, or mandrake, is a thick, fleshy-rooted

plant which yields a narcotic poison and which in ancient
times was believed to resemble the human form and to
shriek when pulled from the ground.)

Chas is not reassured by Turner's explanation.

Chas: I'm going nutty.
Turner: No you're not.
Chas: Am I going nutty?
Pherber: C'mon . . . you're beautiful . . . You're nice
. . . we dismantled you a little bit. That's all.
Turner: Then we can put you together, see? Your
new image.

Cammell posits an almost therapeutic consequence of the
psychedelic experience. His performance 'dismantled',
Chas now sees the world through fresh eyes. His ingrained
antagonisms and prejudices fall away like old skin. He is
transformed from a man of violence to a man capable, for
the first time, of love.

Interestingly, Donald Cammell himself was not particularly partial to drugs, although he smoked hash and had
taken LSD.
Myriam Gibril: 'Donald was so sensitive. He almost had
the sensitivity of a woman to a certain point. There was
that cool, Capricorn exterior, very much in control of his
work; but underneath he was sensitive. He could not take
coke. He took an iota, a pinhead, and he couldn't handle
it. His body was too refined. He had antennae hooked up
on something most people do not.'

E

Edit, The

On completion of filming in late 1968, the fate of *Performance* hung on the shifting balance of power at Warner Bros, the studio which had produced the film. When the deal to make *Performance* was first negotiated and agreed, Warner was owned by Seven Arts, a New York company which had previously specialised in syndicating old movies and cartoons for television, and which had stunned Hollywood in 1966 by purchasing Jack Warner's controlling interest in the film studios for $32m – a takeover which one Warner Bros executive likened to the *Pasadena News* taking over the *New York Times*.

On completion of the film, Ken Hyman, Warner's head of production in London, was opposed to its release. But in 1969, Warner was sold to Steve Ross and his Kinney National Services, a company that had built its fortune on parking lots and funeral parlours but was anxious to move into the entertainment field. The takeover brought Kinney under government scrutiny. Caesar Kimmel, Kinney's executive vice-president and the original owner of Kinney's parking-lot business, was the son of Emmanuel Kimmel, a well-known New Jersey gambler. Ross and Caesar Kimmel had become involved in a gambling case brought by the New York district attorney after Kimmel senior arranged for Kinney limousines to be used to ferry gamblers from New York to New Jersey for a crap game. Caesar Kimmel maintained that his company had nothing to do with running the gambling operation, and no charges were ever filed, but in the wake of the allegations, the Kinney takeover came under close scrutiny.

It was against this background that the new regime at Warner came to re-evaluate *Performance*.

According to Sandy Lieberson, both Ted Ashley, the new chairman of Warner, who had previously worked as an agent for ICM, and John Calley, the head of production, had strong reservations about the film. 'Things were more or less frozen from the time we finished shooting. We were allowed a little money to complete the first stage of the edit. But Warners were threatening never to release it because of the nature of the movie. They were extremely nervous.'

There were even rumours that other studio heads were urging Warner to turn the film over to a small, independent distributor, in order to avoid bringing 'disgrace' to the film industry. But Lieberson found an ally in another executive named Fred Weintraub. Weintraub had previously owned the Bottom Line, a rock venue in New York, and he had persuaded Warner to back the film *Woodstock*. (A film which, interestingly, Warner had no reservations about hurrying into release, reasoning perhaps, that it displayed a more acceptable face of the counter-culture than *Performance* did.) 'Fred was a great and flamboyant character,' says Lieberson. 'I contacted him and he said this sounds like a great movie, let's get it finished. He convinced Calley and Ashley, and he got the film to the point where we could preview it.' The film's original editor had been replaced by Anthony Gibbs, an experienced and well-respected editor who had previously worked on *A Taste of Honey*, *The Loneliness of the Long Distance Runner* and *Tom Jones*. It was Gibbs who executed the first completed cut of the film, which was previewed in Santa Monica in July 1969.

The preview was a disaster. Warner executives thought the film was too long and were outraged by the explicit sex and violence, and the simple fact that Mick Jagger – to their mind, the single largest commercial asset in the film – did not even appear until halfway through. They demanded that the film should be re-edited in Los Angeles, under John Calley's supervision. An interesting insight into what Warner found objectionable can be gleaned from two scenes that Cammell subsequently cut. In the final version, after Harry Flowers has pronounced the death sentence on Chas, we see him about to enter the bathroom, a leering smile on his face. The original version cut away to reveal the object of his aroused anticipation – a naked man. The naked man was cut. So too were a handful of frames from the scene in which Chas shoots Joey Maddocks, which showed a dying Maddocks reaching for a razor blade and slicing Chas's shoe.

Sandy Lieberson: 'Nic had another film to start – *Walkabout*. And I had to come back to London to produce *Mary Queen of Scots*, directed by Sandy McKendrick. So we left Donald in Los Angeles to re-edit the movie. There was a lot of discussion about how the film was to be re-edited, but ultimately we had to leave it in Donald's hands.'

Cammell rejected Warner's first choice of editor to work with him on the film, instead settling on his own choice, an experienced Hollywood editor named Frank Mazzola.

Frank Mazzola: 'As soon as I met Donald there was this immediate rapport, even before I saw the film. I could sense the soul and the spirit in the guy. It wasn't like money and big movies and 'being a director'; this was a guy who was really serious about making films.

'I was told by a guy at Warner Bros that if I did the film I'd be black-balled. I knew it had been on the shelf for a while and there were problems with the show.

'When I saw it for the first time it was beautiful to look at, but it was very slow. Donald was saying, "I want to inter-cut; I want to flash forward. I want to throw away time." He had that whole sensibility that Godard came up with of "beginning, middle and end but not necessarily in that order if it works dramatically". So I felt compelled to do it.

'We started work in the old Sam Goldwyn studios in Hollywood, working from seven at night till five in the morning. I got separate dialogue, effects and music tracks, because I wanted to cut everything against the picture, to give it that meter we had.

'Donald was extremely articulate, in a very English way. He liked to talk a lot in the editing-room. He'd pick up a book and start reading – Borges or something like that – and then he'd come over and look at what was going on and start talking and the energy would rise. I would be cutting and all of a sudden the film would just take over. It was like stepping into a world of magic. Things would start flying through my hands. I could feel the electricity in the film going through my teeth. The film took on its own life and I was trying to chase it. Everything we tried worked.

'The whole edit was about throwing time away; cutting forwards and backwards. And there's dialogue things we did, starting a line of dialogue in one sequence and finishing in another . . . like when Chas goes into the office and starts ripping things off the wall, the words start in his mouth and end up in the lawyer's mouth in the courtroom. We didn't think about those things too much; they just happened.

'The bulk of my work was done in the first half of the film. Warners couldn't figure out how this was a film that starred Mick Jagger and you didn't see him for the first half of the film; they wanted to get to him sooner. So we moved him up, just symbolically, with that shot of him spray-painting the wall. That seemed to satisfy them.

'To me, what *Performance* became was the first MTV film. I was watching *Shallow Grave* and they do that flash-forward editing. Everybody does it nowadays. But we were obviously doing it too soon.

'I thought *Performance* was going to tear Hollywood down and open up the doors. It was just the reverse for me. People in the studios didn't want to touch me after I'd worked on the film. They thought it was nuts. They didn't understand it at all. But they never do.'

*   *   *

Sandy Lieberson: 'The final edit caused some differences of opinion between Donald and Nic and myself – perhaps more with Nic, because as co-director he had a more proprietorial interest in the film. The re-edit that Donald did, another kind of film emerged – the same material, but a different structure; the editing technique evolved and so on.

'I think all of us had been very committed to the film that had been previewed, the length of the film and the structure of the film; it was a more classic structure, and in the way it made the story a little bit stronger. The character of James Fox was very delineated; and Harry Flowers and all this peripheral homosexual, violent underworld scene in London was explored in greater depth. That was something that all of us thought was terribly important that hadn't ever been revealed before in a British film. But that had to be truncated in the edited version of the film. I would say twenty minutes was taken out. And Nic wasn't very happy with that.'

Donald Cammell: 'Nic Roeg disliked the final cut. He was very upset. He said, I want to take my name off the movie. He denies it now, because he went around getting credit for the film for years, which really pissed me off. He pissed on the cut.'

Sandy Lieberson: 'I don't ever recall having ever heard Nic ask to remove his name from the film. I think it's one of these stories that developed out of the competitive nature between Donald and Nic after the film. It may have been Donald's projection that Nic wanted that. But

I don't think he seriously, or formally, asked to have his name taken off.'

End, The

Chas climbs the stairs of 81 Powis Square and enters Turner's bedroom, to bid his adieus.

'I might come with you, then,' says Turner.

'You don't know where I'm going, pal,' Chas replies.

Turner regards him implacably. 'I do.'

Chas pauses, moves around the bed. This lacuna sows a moment's doubt in Turner's mind. 'I don't know . . .'

'Yeah, you do . . .' says Chas.

Chas, as we know, is going to his death. And Turner knows this too. Death is Chas's gift to Turner, the final assassin's act for which Turner and Pherber earlier prepared him. There is something animistic at work here; just as the tribesman believes that he appropriates the spirit of the animal he kills, so too may Chas appropriate Turner's spirit, and in so doing release the singer from the bondage of his own inertia.

In this way, the two have become one. We know that it is Chas who is led out to Harry Flowers's car, *en route* to his execution, but the face that turns to look out at us from the back of the car is Turner's.

The final shot of the film shows Harry Flowers's Rolls driving along a country lane, although it seems that even after completing the film Cammell and Roeg wanted to go further. Cammell wrote to Lieberson pleading for a chance to re-shoot the ending, showing the Rolls driving through New York's Central Park, the camera panning back to show the Manhattan skyline – Chas delivered at last to the promised land of his imagination. That idea never came to fruition, and the film instead closes on a freeze-shot of the promised land described by Lucy, the spiritual home of bandits and assassins – the mountains of Persia.

Evans, Jimmy

According to Donald Cammell, the character of Chas was substantially modelled on George 'Jimmy' Evans, an East End criminal who was introduced to Cammell by David Litvinoff, the man credited as 'director of authenticity' on *Performance*.

Evans gained public notoriety for his involvement in the killing of Thomas 'Ginger' Marks, a car dealer and minor-league villain, who was shot down in an East London street in 1965. Marks's body was abducted, and never found. Underworld rumours had it that he had either been dumped in a gravel pit or buried in a motorway pillar.

Jimmy Evans was at Marks's side when he was shot. In 1975, Evans was released from prison, where he was serving a seven-year sentence on a separate charge of manslaughter, to give evidence at the Old Bailey against the four men accused of Marks's murder. Among the accused was Frederick Foreman.

The Old Bailey jury was told that Evans, 'a violent man', had allegedly shot Foreman's brother, George, with a double-barrelled twelve-bore shotgun which he had borrowed from Marks, in an argument over Evans's wife. Evans, described as a 'fruit machine proprietor', stood trial for the shooting in 1965, but was acquitted.

Frederick Foreman and the three other men charged with the murder of Thomas Marks were subsequently acquitted.

'Jimmy was a great rapper,' Cammell remembered. 'Very funny, very cold, very intense. And very entertaining.'

F

Fifty

The age at which Turner, according to Chas, will look 'funny'. The line 'You'll look funny when you're fifty' was later sampled by English rock group Big Audio Dynamite and used in their homage to Nic Roeg, 'E=MC2', to be found on the group's 1985 album *This is Big Audio Dynamite*.

Flowers, Harry

Boss of the London gang for whom Chas works as an enforcer, Harry Flowers was a type of gangster who had never been seen in British cinema before *Performance*; the authentic voice of the London criminal underworld (his voice, literally, so authentic that Warner made the bizarre and absurd decision to over-dub Shannon's dialogue for the American release of the film, reasoning that American audiences would have trouble understanding him), a man painted in altogether more subtle colours than the crude cinematic stereotype of the ruthless 'Mr Big'.

To understand Harry Flowers, it is necessary to understand the changing complexion of organised crime in London in the 1960s. The gangsters and toughs who had ruled the London underworld of illegal gaming, prostitution and protection in the pre- and post-war periods were giving way to a new and more sophisticated sort of criminal who cloaked his activities under the veneer of legitimate business.

The Krays in the East End of London, and their South London counterparts, the Richardsons, styled their gangs as 'firms' and themselves as 'businessmen' ('company director' was the preferred euphemism for any self-respecting villain making an appearance in court or the newspaper columns).

The court-case which opens *Performance* suggests that Flowers has his fingers in any number of pies. A former politician, 'a leader of men in days of national peril', as Harley-Brown puts it, stands accused of fraud, and is threatening to drag into the case the name of his erstwhile partner, Flowers.

In court, the barrister Harley-Brown argues for 'the inalienable right of the smaller business to be conjoined in commercial union with an expansionist-minded association or group of companies'. Out of court, equipment is ripped off the walls of a mini-cab firm, and a dustbin crashes through the window of a betting-shop.

'Business is business and progress is progress,' Harley-Brown lectures the jury. 'Our national economy, even our national survival, devolves upon the consolidation by merger of the smaller and weaker economic units with the larger and lustier pillars of the commercial complex.'

Flowers uses exactly the same justification in bringing the book-maker Joey Maddocks into line. 'It's not a takeover. It's a merger' because 'small businesses in this day and age is against nature'.

Cammell artfully juxtaposes these arguments to make

the point that the predatory world of 'legitimate' business and the world of violent crime are two sides of the same coin – equally corrupt, equally self-serving. And the jury in the fraud case are as much duped spectators as the audience in the blue-movie cinema, whose Cypriot proprietor Chas terrorises.

This theme of merger is, of course, echoed later in the film in the relationship between Chas and Turner, but here the merger is not one founded on duplicity or violence but on a self-knowledge grounded in the revelations of the drug experience and sexual honesty.

Flowers and his 'firm' are beautifully observed: thugs who disguise their venality and sadism under a thin veneer of gentrified respectability, which Cammell and Roeg suggest by a dazzling accumulation of small detail: Flowers conducts his business under the comfort of a quilted eiderdown, or to the soothing strains of Muzak ('Turn it up. I like that . . .'); his office is a parody of the St James's gentleman's club (the sort of club of which Harley-Brown is a member), with its leather Chesterfield, the marble bust on the sideboard, the *faux* hunting prints on the wall. As they go about their business of terror, Chas, Moody and Rosenbloom enact an ongoing charade of addressing each other with exaggerated politesse – 'That, Mr Brownjohn, is what I call a nice short back and sides.' 'One of your best efforts, Mr Peel . . .' Rosebloom fastidiously squirts breath-freshener into his mouth. Everybody dresses soberly in suits and ties, as if for a day at the office. (Ronnie Kray insisted on a similar dress-code for his henchmen: 'I like conservative clothes,' he once said. 'I can't stand anybody flash.')

Perhaps the most obvious departure from the cinema conventions of the gangster is the fact that Flowers is homosexual – an aspect of his character which is clearly modelled on Ronnie Kray – a bold recognition by the film-makers of the covert strain of homoeroticism which underpins the ostensibly 'masculine' pursuits of boxing, body-building and the male-bonding of the criminal gang.

Johnny Shannon, who played Flowers, had met the Krays 'when I was a little kid', but claims to have based his character on a number of characters from south of the river. 'I knew the Richardsons. I've never been a gangster, but because I lived in South London I knew lots of them.'

He says that he accepted the role without fully realising that Flowers was supposed to be homosexual. 'They made it all into a joke at first, see,' Shannon told the *Guardian* in 1971. 'In the script it just said that Harry Flowers was "a businessman of effeminate nature". I just accepted that. It didn't really strike me until there's this scene where I'm shaving, and there's this boy running my bath with nothing on but a towel around his middle. Then I look at him, and I smile. Then I saw it all, I doubled up.

'The chaps used to have a little nobble at me about playing a pouf.'

Fox, James (b. 1939)

At the time of making *Performance*, James Fox was the most gilded, and certainly the most electrifying young actor on the British screen, the closest thing Britain had to a genuine world-class star in the making.

The son of a well-known theatrical agent, Robin Fox, James – or William, as he was christened – was subject to a classic English upper-middle-class upbringing: prep-school, Harrow, and a spell as a junior officer in the Coldstream Guards during National Service, which included service in Kenya. His father's connections with the theatrical world drew him naturally to acting. His first film role, in *The Loneliness of the Long Distance Runner*, was quickly followed by a breakthrough part in Joseph Losey's adaptation of the Harold Pinter script, *The Servant*, playing a weak-willed young aristocrat who is manipulated by his manservant (Dirk Bogarde). *Those Magnificent Men in Their Flying Machines*, *King Rat*, *Isadora* and *Thoroughly Modern Millie* followed, all reinforcing Fox's film 'type' as the strait-laced, upper-class and cut-glass-vowelled Englishman. In person, however, Fox had begun to breathe something of the spirit of the times. A Californian girlfriend introduced him to marijuana, and his social orbit began to shift towards the more raffish fringes of film, pop and aristo-bohemia. 'I was in that slightly druggy, slightly rock and roll environment,' he would later recall. 'I suppose I was a rather privileged hippie.'

For a while he lived in Rome, driving around the streets in a 3.8-litre Jaguar with a built-in record player blaring out Arthur Conley and Sam and Dave songs. He also made the obligatory pilgrimage to Morocco, smoking copious amounts of kif and sampling the powerful hallucinogen STP.

The popular myth about Fox and *Performance* is that the film somehow 'blew his mind', and was the principal reason for him retiring from acting and taking up Christian evangelism. But in his autobiography, *Comeback*, published in 1983, Fox suggests that he had begun to feel serious disquiet about the direction in which his life was heading long before the film was made. 'Not only was I in a guilty muddle about drugs,' Fox writes of his time in Rome, 'but my sexual imagination was also in complete turmoil.'

In April 1967 he confided to his diary: 'I am in the grip of a fearful realisation which frightens me even now of the wasteful, evil life into which I have let myself fall. I, who would five years ago have looked at my present situation with compassion and anxiety, am now in a pre-planned hell which has come upon me like a creeping black plague which contaminates the victim without apparently affecting him but which gives his friends and others horrible intimations of the most probable end towards which he must go. I was driven here mostly out of loneliness and out of admiration for what looked exciting but which is dangerous. The way to happiness is not found on the youthful trips of crazy imaginations.'

He writes that he made the resolution to study the New Testament – 'but meanwhile life in Rome was getting more diverting. The Rolling Stones, who were making a European tour, came to Rome and through going to their concert with the Gettys we met Mick Jagger, Brian Jones and the rest . . .'

His meeting with Jagger led Fox into the charmed circle of London's hippie *jeunesse dorée* – the Stones, Anita

Pallenberg, Robert Fraser, Christopher Gibbs and Donald Cammell. Fox and his girlfriend, Andee Cohen, became particularly close to Jagger and his girlfriend, Marianne Faithfull.

In her autobiography, Faithfull recalls meeting Fox and Cohen at a party hosted by Dirk Bogarde at the Connaught Hotel in London. Faithfull writes that it was actually Andee Cohen who first caught her eye – 'an exquisite little thing, a vivid, fluttering creature, very thin and androgynous, with dark hair cut short like a boy's and big, big eyes'. Faithfull and Jagger, Fox and Cohen – the four quickly became inseparable, whiling away the evenings at Jagger's Cheyne Walk house in a haze of music and mind-altering substances. It was a curious friendship in which the louche pop star would constantly tease the upper-middle-class actor about his accent and manners, but it blossomed, in Donald Cammell's phrase, into 'a little romance'.

Fox and Cammell would work together on the film *Duffy*. It was not, Fox recalls in *Comeback*, a particularly happy experience, but it cemented his friendship with Cammell, and while Fox took off for a recreational trip up the Amazon, Cammell turned his attention to the script of *Performance*, with Fox now firmly in mind for the character of Chas.

Sandy Lieberson: 'Both Donald and I liked James as a person, and saw something in him that hadn't really surfaced – except perhaps in *The Servant* – in what he'd been doing previously. He'd been playing rather innocuous parts. We thought there was something in his character that would be interesting in this kind of role, casting him against type. And what we didn't want to do was get hung up with movie stars. It was going to be difficult enough with Mick Jagger. We thought if we could recruit someone to the project who was going to be as committed and as enthusiastic as we were, rather than somebody who would be hired, so to speak, it would make our life a lot easier. And James loved the idea of playing that kind of a character. It was something he would never have been offered to do otherwise.'

Fox's father, Robin, who had long had anxieties about his son's lifestyle, had reservations about the film.

Sandy Lieberson: 'Robin was part of the establishment, absolutely. He was a director of the Royal Court theatre. He was a theatre producer as well as being an agent. He was a rather grand and very intelligent man; extremely worldly and courteous. He had no real objection at first. But I think he became worried later as the project became a reality and he saw what the subject matter was. And I think he became concerned with James's involvement with drugs and this whole scene of people who he felt might have been corrupting or have some negative influence on James.

'He didn't do anything to block the project, but he did ultimately try to dissuade James from doing it. I don't think he thought it was a good career move. And in a way his alarm was justified. James was pretty close to going off the rails in his own life. His father's instinct about his son was absolutely right. And it wasn't long afterwards that Robin died, and that created a terrible upset for James because I don't know whether he'd resolved his relationship with his father.'

Fox would later describe the role of Chas as the best he has ever played. It is hard to imagine anyone else in the role. Through David Litvinoff he was introduced to Johnny Shannon, a sometime market trader and boxing trainer, who was charged with tutoring the actor in the manners and mores of the South London criminal world, introducing him to 'the chaps' and knocking the polish off his Harrovian accent and genteel manners. Through the writer Francis Wyndham he was introduced to Ronnie Kray, and on one occasion he was played a tape of an anonymous gangster recalling his part in a revenge killing.

Fox took a small flat in Brixton, and began training at the Thomas A' Beckett gym in the Old Kent Road. He cropped his hair, bought a handful of suits from Cecil Gee, and, along with Shannon, began doing the rounds of pubs and spielers, taking on the part of the aspirant South London hoodlum with a relish that some found disquieting. David Cammell remembers Fox coming into the production office in Chelsea one day with a gripe, banging his fist on the table and 'terrifying the secretaries'. Cammell says that on another occasion he received a telephone call from a worried Johnny Shannon saying that 'the boy' had been out on some business the previous night involving a stolen car, although both Shannon and Fox have denied that Fox was ever involved in any criminal activities.

'I became almost completely taken over by the role,' Fox recalled in *Comeback*. 'I spoke, thought and ate like Chas.' It even affected his choice of girlfriend. For a short time he went out with Ann Sidney, who played the part of Chas's girlfriend, Dana.

The conflict between the confused 'privileged hippie'
Fox, and the role he was playing as Chas, was to have a
marked effect on him as the shooting moved from the
West End gangster scenes to the claustrophobic confines
of the Lowndes Square set (where most of *Performance*
was shot), exacerbated by his relationships with Jagger
and Pallenberg (see **The Shoot**).

Writing fifteen years later in *Comeback*, Fox would take
a curiously sanguine view of the themes of *Performance*.

> The film's sexual content reflected the times and
> my own previous experiences – the idea that one
> could find gentleness and friendship through sex,
> that sex was not a macho aggressive rugby-club
> knock. The conventional identity attitudes, that
> the film makers believed, were more cultural and
> inherited than truthful. I was sympathetic to those
> ideas in 1969 [sic], although their consequences were
> by then producing pain and confusion in my life and
> the lives of my close friends.

Of the tensions and difficulties with Jagger and Pallenberg
during the shoot, Fox's book makes no mention, referring
only to a 'slight disagreement' with Donald Cammell over
the characterisation of Chas.

> Could Turner and Pherber really have believed that
> they could discover the source of the mystery of
> Chas' personality and talent by dressing him up
> as an Arabian assassin and feeding him fly-agaric
> mushrooms? If they did think that, then I felt

that made the character a bit naïve. Because of this slight disagreement I found the last few weeks of the film less enjoyable, but we finished more or less on schedule and all of us felt it had been a great experience.

For Fox, it was to prove a life-changing one. In *Comeback*, he notes that 'the effect the film had on me was really to turn me from drugs as a means of self-discovery and spiritual discovery and from the free and uninhibited use of sex as a means of seeking permanent happiness. I don't mean to say that I rejected sex, but just the way I had been using it. Cutting myself away from these things left a vacuum, especially by separating me from the friends I enjoyed. The film and the part of Chas had already contributed to that.'

His friendship with Jagger also came to an end. 'The role of Chas – becoming that person – was so strongly antithetical to the role that Mick had played that we couldn't make it back together,' he later recalled. 'Or perhaps we just moved apart. I felt I'd moved from it, and it was a positive move.'

Fox began attending church and decided to concentrate on theatre work. A year after *Performance*, in Blackpool, where he was performing in *Doctor in the House*, he struck up conversation with a man named Bernie Marks, who told Fox he had come to Blackpool to 'spend a day with the Lord'. It was a meeting that led to Fox joining a Christian movement called the Navigators and leaving acting for ten years to concentrate on evangelism, before eventually making a tentative return to film and television work.

He would later recall the years following *Performance* as a period of 'major conflicts and tensions, because I could not reconcile my previous wild life with something that was wholly new and positive in so many ways. It was very confusing for a while, but it's better now.' He continues to regard *Performance* as 'one of the most important British films ever made'.

G

Genet, Jean (1910–86)

Donald Cammell was introduced to the works of the novelist Jean Genet, France's most celebrated criminal of letters, while living in Paris in the mid-Sixties, and became deeply enamoured of Genet's vivid and poetic descriptions of the criminal underworld. Genet's book *The Thief's Journal* was to be particularly influential on Cammell: he was so impressed by it that he gave copies to both Jagger and Fox as part of their preparation for *Performance*.

Genet was born in Paris, an illegitimate child, abandoned by his parents whom he never knew. Fostered to a peasant family in Le Morvan, he embarked on a life of crime, stealing, according to his friend and biographer Jean-Paul Sartre, to compensate for the fact that he was the only person in the village who had no possessions of his own. Sartre regarded Genet's criminal activities as an 'existentialist choice'. After being imprisoned in a juvenile reformatory at Mettray, he embarked on a peripatetic journey through the criminal underworld of Europe, living by theft and male prostitution and spending frequent periods in prison. Genet wrote his first novel, *Notre Dame des Fleurs*, in 1942. A year later, he was sentenced to life imprisonment, but was granted a pardon after appeals from a quorum of French writers and intellectuals.

Journal du Voleur – *The Thief's Journal* – written in 1949, is essentially autobiographical, describing the narrator's wanderings through Europe in the company of hoodlums, pimps and petty criminals. The book is extraordinary not only for its unflinching candour, but also for Genet's capacity to find beauty and heroism in a world of unrelenting squalor and degradation.

In his outline for *The Performers*, Cammell borrows from *The Thief's Journal* to describe the character of Chas, the criminal as existentialist hero:

> He's a criminal, a young thug, who's been picked for this key job by the professionals who run the business because he is what he is. In the first pages of *The Thief's Journal*, Jean Genet describes to perfection the essence of his kind:

> *Crime, I said to myself, had a long wait before producing such perfect successes as Pilorge and Angel Sun . . . it was necessary that a host of circumstances concur: to the handsomeness of their faces, to the strength and elegance of their bodies there had to be added their taste for crime, the circumstances which make the criminal, the moral vigour capable of accepting such a destiny, and finally, punishment, its cruelty, the intrinsic quality which enables a criminal to glory in it.*

In a sociologist's view, psychopaths [Cammell continues in his notes]. But it is equally true that Mr Genet's vision is equally true, if not truer. Of course, he loved young men like this with a pure and powerful love. Possibly this is where it is, to coin a phrase, at. In any case Genet takes for granted the essence of Chas: which is, not to be violent, but to be violence. (Not to kill – a gun going off; but to threaten death – a loaded gun.)

I give the name violence to a boldness lying idle and hankering for danger . . . It unnerves you. This violence is a calm that disturbs you. One sometimes says 'A guy with class'. Pilorge's delicate features were of an extreme violence. Their delicacy in particular was violent . . . Even when at rest, motionless and smiling, there escaped from them through the eyes, the nostrils, the mouth, the palm of the hand . . . a radiant and sombre anger visible as a haze.

The Thief's Journal offers an aesthetic and philosophical inspiration for *Performance* rather than a textual one, although there is one observation in the book which resonates in the final assassination of Turner by Chas – and in Cammell's own decision thirty years later to take his own life.

'Acts,' Genet writes, 'must be carried through to their completion. Whatever their point of departure, the end will be beautiful. It is because an action has not been completed that it is vile.'

Gibbs, Christopher

Aesthete, antiquarian and designer of Turner's home in *Performance*, Christopher Gibbs was crucial in establishing not only the look of the film, but the aesthetic sensibility of the London scene which gave birth to it.

Long before *Performance*, Gibbs had been a central component in the Chelsea set of the 1950s, a loose aggregate of young aristos, public schoolboys and the more racy species of débutante, who frequented the Markham Arms in the King's Road, and whose principal enthusiasms were clothes, inebriation and a rather self-conscious slumming.

Gibbs was the dandy *par excellence*. In his definitive book on British style in the Sixties, *Today There Are No Gentlemen*, Nik Cohn describes Gibbs as a pupil at Eton, sporting a monocle and a silver-topped cane with blue tassels, handing out visiting-cards. Expelled from Eton, he moved on to the Sorbonne in Paris, returning to London in 1956. As an eighteen-year-old, 'He was very flash. Sometimes he just wore tight jeans or fancy dress, like the others; but mostly his tastes were more elaborate: suits with double-breasted waistcoats and cloth-coloured buttons, and velvet ties, and striped Turkish shirts with stiff white collars, and cravats. Above all, he had a passion for carnations and was forever buying new strains, pink-and-yellow, or green-ink, or purple with red flecks.'

In 1959, Gibbs opened a shop in Chelsea, selling antique clothes and objects. He was among the first of London's proto-hippies to travel to Morocco, returning with drapes, hangings, cushions and jewellery. Other travellers were heading east on the hippie trail – to Persia, the Hindu Kush and India – and returning with similar artefacts. This exotic mixture of Eastern and North African decorative arts and trappings would come to define the well-heeled boho-hippie style so prevalent at the time *Performance* was filmed.

It was this style which Gibbs employed in designing Brian Jones's flat at 1 Courtfield Road in Earls Court, and which Donald Cammell had in mind for Turner's Notting Hill house. In his treatment for 'The Performers', Cammell specifies that Turner's bedroom should be 'decorated predominantly in the Gibbsian Moroccan manner, furnished with strange and beautiful things'.

It is clear from this that Cammell had a clear sense in his own mind of exactly what Turner's surroundings should look like, the picture they should convey of the rock star's enthusiasms and predilections. His bedroom, Cammell writes, is 'littered with multifarious stuff, with books, records, antique clothes and oriental objects of religious significance. The room, like the house, like its owner, seduces one with the glamour of its decay – an almost archaeological patina. The dust in its crannies is of a refined sensibility.'

The 'Big Room', where Turner encounters Chas for the first time, is also vividly described: 'Part furnished, part carpeted, part painted, but nevertheless complete. A great part of it is gaunt, empty-looking; another is a closed-in sepulchre of mattresses and cushions. There are bare patches where big paintings have come down to be re-sold. A chandelier (next to go?), a piano, an organ (and a mellotron?) ... musical instruments from recondite cultures ... maps ... a pile of stones ... a maze of shallow, shattered mirrors ... mysteries, banalities, old newspapers, a tank of sluggish carp through which sunlight trickles, polarising the dust.'

This is a setting where everything is both half-familiar and deeply strange, a household of marvels, magical effects and illusions. We see the place through Chas's eyes, disorientated by the way in which rooms seem to change their size, their shape, their appearance, the way figures chimerically appear and disappear from behind curtains, in mirrors.

Gibbs's interiors are crucial in creating this sense of an enclosed world – a mausoleum almost – which is Turner's redoubt against the vagaries of his own fame, the reality of his abandoned career and, at the same time, utterly alienating to Chas. It is a world where the normal rules no longer apply, an appropriate setting for the unfolding drama as Turner and Pherber dismantle Chas's performance.

Christopher Gibbs: 'I got a lot of things in Morocco; mats and hangings, and gaudy covers for the bed, which had layers and layers of mattresses like "The Princess and the Pea", festooned with sashes and cords and drapes and a bedspread from the Hindu Kush. The bath was marbled, with seventeenth-century Japanese dishes, the tiles designed from a Persian carpet.

'I wanted something mysterious and beautiful and unexpected, exotic and voluptuous and far away from pedestrian; some hint of earthly paradise. It also had to be done in four and a half minutes on four and a half pennies.'

H

Harley-Brown

The barrister who threatens to drag Harry Flowers's name into a potentially damaging court-case, and who, in turn, is threatened by Chas, Rosebloom and Moody.

> *Harley-Brown*: Now listen to me, whatever your name is — I must insist you address your remarks to me . . .
> *Chas*: Address my remarks . . . okey dokey . . . why not, Mr Butler? We have got his address, haven't we?

Harley-Brown's role in the film is not simply as a potential nemesis of Harry Flowers, but as the most obvious symbol of the social and political establishment. The encounter with Chas on the steps of Harley-Brown's club is a powerful metaphor for the burgeoning self-assurance of the working-class, determined no longer to be cowed by their social betters.

> *Harley-Brown*: This is outrageous . . . Are you threatening my client?
> *Chas*: You bet I am, poncey . . .

Chas himself embodies this new spirit of aggressive self-confidence. His sharp suits, camel-hair overcoat and white

Jaguar are symbols of the new upwardly mobile criminal class – ostentatiously flush, but too cool to be flash.

Cammell wrote an early version of *Performance* entitled *The Performers*, in which this class conflict is even more vividly dramatised. In this draft Harley-Brown is not defending a client who is threatening to expose Flowers, but someone who owes Flowers a gambling debt. Chas is sent to recover the money, ambushes Harley-Brown on the steps of his club (the Garrick) and, to Harley-Brown's mounting alarm, follows him inside. Here, in the very heart of the British establishment, all of Chas's suppressed class hostility is given full vent. Harley-Brown tries to lecture Chas on a point of law: 'A debt – an alleged debt – incurred in a game of chance is not enforceable in law. So . . .' But he is shouted down by Chas. 'I got nothing against thieves, mind you – I've got respect for a good thief. A straight criminal. A performer. Such as myself. It's the others what aggravates me. (Looming around room . . . portraits, books – lawyers.) Your lot.'

> *Harley-Brown*: Er . . . I'm not with you, I'm afraid . . .
> *Chas*: The secrets in those poxy books. The lousy keep-it-in-the-family bastards. It's all lies. What-they-call-it . . . you know what I mean? I can smell them. Poncing politicians – stinking parasite businessmen . . . lawyers . . . Do you know what I mean, Brown?'
> *Harley-Brown* (haughty): I can't say I do, Mr Devlin.

Chas concludes the exchange with the ultimate threat.

Glancing around the Garrick he tells Harley-Brown: 'I look forward to joining, I can tell you (leans closer to BROWN. In a whisper; smiling nod). Now you're afraid, eh?'

There could be no more powerful metaphor for the vandals beating at the gates of the most cherished institutions of the upper class, and it's a pity the scene was not included in the film.

The character of Turner illustrates another twist on this idea of the shifting sands of the class-structure. We know nothing of his social background, but we can assume that, like Mick Jagger, Turner is a child of the lower-middle class. But, consistent with the way in which rock stars had become the new aristocracy, he affects the languid air and mannerisms of a stoned peer of the realm. One can only imagine Cammell's wry pleasure at the way Jagger played the role so effectively it seemed to stick to him like glue thereafter; and his sense of vindication at his decision to play one more trick on the subject of class by casting James Fox, an actor who had made his name playing upper-class types, as the working-class hoodlum.

J

Jagger, Mick (b. 1943)

In casting Mick Jagger in the role of Turner, Donald Cammell was calling upon the services of not only the most famous, and most charismatic, rock singer in the world, but also the most notorious. To the British media, and huge swathes of the public, Jagger was the face of degeneracy, the personification of rock music as a threat to moral probity and order.

By 1968, five years after the release of their first single, the Rolling Stones could properly claim to be the greatest rock and roll band in the world. Their great rivals the Beatles might have been more commercially successful, even more musically accomplished, but it was the Stones who most embodied the promise of sexual freedom and cultural insurrection implicit in rock music – an index not only of musical possibilities but of social ones too.

If Keith Richard personified a kind of steely, outlaw toughness, and Brian Jones a foppish decadence – a rare orchid wilting from a surfeit of attention and excess – Jagger posited an altogether more flagrant challenge to the values of the day. His unapologetic narcissism – the pouting, voluptuous lips, the animal grace of his gestures – lay somewhere beyond received ideas of sexuality, at a point which was neither masculine nor feminine. Quite simply, he *was* sex.

Reflecting on the figure of Jagger today – a multi-millionaire father of five, best known for his apparently indefatigable enthusiasm for young models – it is hard to consider the figure of outrage he cut in the Sixties, hounded by the Establishment and vilified in the press.

The Stones' biographer, Philip Norman, tells the story of Jagger and his girlfriend Marianne Faithfull arriving at Heathrow in 1967 and being unable to find a taxi that would accept their fare. Sentenced to imprisonment that year for the illegal possession of amphetamines (see **Mars Bars**), Jagger became the subject of a leader article in *The Times*, arguing his cause. When the sentence was quashed on appeal, he famously appeared on television's *World in Action* – that lisping voice, the hand casually sweeping the hair from his eyes – the subject of rapt attention from such Establishment worthies as William Rees-Mogg, the Bishop of Woolwich and the former Home Secretary Lord Stow-Hill, all hanging on Jagger's every word as he pontificated on the perplexing question of 'yoof'.

Of all the Stones it was Jagger who responded most readily to the possibilities of social mobility the age provided. He glided between the worlds of rock, art, high society and public life (the Labour MP Tom Driberg even tried to persuade him to pursue a career in politics) – an evanescent, dilettantish figure, curiously located beyond the bounds of class or gender.

There is one Rolling Stones song of this period which, more than any other, seems to embody Jagger. Its opening stanza, sneered as much as sung over a voodoo beat – 'Please allow me to introduce myself, I'm a man of wealth and taste' – has the calculated ring of autobiography. It is, of course, a song about Lucifer.

'Sympathy for the Devil' had sprung indirectly from another of Jagger's acquaintances of the time, the film-maker, student of Aleister Crowley and magician, Kenneth Anger.

The son of an aeronautics engineer, Anger grew up in Hollywood. His grandmother had been a wardrobe mistress for United Artists in the days of the silents, and it was through her offices that Anger made his first appearance on film at the age of four, playing the part of the 'changeling prince' in Max Reinhardt's 1936 version of *A Midsummer Night's Dream*, scampering in spangles and plumes through an enchanted forest thrown up on the backlot of Warner's studios.

Seduced by his grandmother's backstage tittle-tattle about the Hollywood stars – 'my Grimms' fairy-tales' – Anger became a devotee and a historian of Hollywood's darker secrets. These were later to find their way into print in two volumes of *Hollywood Babylon*.

Anger became obsessed with movie-making, making his first film, *Who's Rocking My Dreamboat*, at the age of eleven, using stock left over from his family's holiday movies. Five years later he made his first exhibited film, *Fireworks*, a startlingly precocious homoerotic fantasy, shot in three days with his grandmother's connivance, while his parents were away.

Jean Cocteau saw the film and invited Anger to Paris, where he made *Puce Moment*, *Eaux d'Artifice* and an unfinished adaptation of the erotic novel *L'histoire d'O*. Returning to America, Anger consolidated his reputation

as one of the foremost avant-garde film-makers with
Scorpio Rising, a homoerotic paean to biker-culture, which
intercut footage from Marlon Brando's *The Wild One* with
images of Christ, as seen in a third-rate Hollywood Biblical
epic, over teenbeat hymns like 'He's A Rebel' and 'My
Boyfriend's Back'.

Anger described his films as 'magickal spells', inspired
by his other abiding enthusiasm, for the life and work
of Aleister Crowley. (He wore Crowley's seal, '666',
the number of the Beast from the Book of Revelations,
tattooed on his forearm.) Anger had been introduced
to Crowley's teachings by the widow of Jack Parsons,
a physicist whom Crowley, it was said, had anointed
to carry on his work after his death. In 1955, Anger
made a pilgrimage to Crowley's 'Abbey of Thelema'
in Sicily, to restore the ritualistic wall-painting which
had been whitewashed over by Mussolini's police after
Crowley's departure. Local peasants, suspecting a revival of
Crowleyism, greeted him with the traditional island curse
– a dead cat on the doorstep; a greeting Anger apparently
accepted with characteristic phlegmatism, leaving three
months later when his work was completed.

Anger was a frequent visitor to London in the Sixties.
A fascinating, if sometimes disconcerting, presence, his
all-pervasive air of mystery and his exotic enthusiams made
him a welcome guest in the soirées at Brian Jones's flat in
Courtfield Road and Robert Fraser's in Mount Street.
Anita Pallenberg recalls a weekend at Keith Richard's
country home, Redlands. 'I remember looking out of
the window at dawn . . . we had this target for archery,
and Kenneth was running around in circles with a dog

and a cat, and I thought, "Wow, this is very strange stuff . . .'' At one stage, Anita and Keith were reportedly contemplating a pagan marriage ceremony with Anger officiating, but evidently thought better of it.

In their fascination with the darker elements of sexuality and violence, their Crowleyan invocation of magic, Anger's films can be seen as a direct precursor to, and a significant influence on, *Performance*. Indeed, Donald Cammell admitted that Anger was '*the* major influence at the time I made *Performance*', and that a lot of elements in the film were 'directly attributable' to the American film-maker.

Anger was particularly close to Marianne Faithfull and Mick Jagger, drawn to the ritualistic power of the rock star's performance. It was Anger who first introduced Marianne to *The Master and Margarita*, Mikhail Bulgakov's satire about the Devil's impromptu arrival on the streets of Moscow, which was to become the inspiration for Jagger's song 'Sympathy for the Devil'.

Anger's long-running project was the film *Lucifer Rising*, an apologia for the fallen angel, in which Anger intended 'to restore Lucifer to his rightful position as the bringer of light'.

The film had a chequered and unfortunate history. An early candidate for the role of Lucifer was Bobby Beausoleil, a one-time member of the group Love, with whom Anger was involved, but who was fired after he started to behave 'like demons in people do'. Beausoleil took his revenge by stealing most of the footage of the film. He was later to become involved with Charles Manson's 'Family' and be imprisoned for life for murder, from where he continued to correspond with Anger, signing himself 'Lucifer'.

Anger tried, without success, to persuade Jagger to take over the role, although the singer did agree to provide a Moog synthesiser soundtrack for a segment of *Lucifer Rising*, which was later exhibited under the title *Invocation of My Demon Brother* (1969). Jagger was, allegedly, so unnerved by the whole experience that, according to Anger, he took to wearing a crucifix for months afterwards.

Jagger's appearance in *Performance*, and his relationship on set with Anita Pallenberg, threatened to drive a wedge into the most important partnership within the Stones – that of Jagger and his closest friend, songwriting partner – and Pallenberg's lover – Keith Richard. Sandy Lieberson found himself cast in the role of intermediary and peace-maker.

> At the end of the movie, in talking to Mick, he wanted to find some project that would heal the breach and bring the Stones closer together. They couldn't tour. Mick was going off to Australia to do *Ned Kelly*. So we came up with the idea of doing a television special, 'The Rolling Stones Rock and Roll Circus', which we did soon after the end of *Performance*.

After that, things began to fall apart. In July 1969, Brian Jones drowned in the swimming-pool of his Sussex home. The Stones played their free Hyde Park concert in his memory (Jagger in a silk shift dress from Mr Fish, reciting Shelley and releasing butterflies from a box – most of which appeared to have already expired from suffocation). Jagger departed for Australia to make his second film, *Ned Kelly*. It was there that Marianne Faithfull attempted suicide, the prelude to her own descent into heroin addiction. Later that same year came what many would come to see as the horrible culmination of the Stones' flirtation with the forces of violence: the Altamont festival, where Hell's Angels, who had been employed as the festival security force, stabbed to death eighteen-year-old Meredith Hunter only yards from where the Stones were performing. Staring into the face of authentic horror, Jagger seemed to metamorphose from the Prince of Darkness into a small, frightened creature, the cocksure sneer reduced to a pathetic cry for order: 'People ... who's fightin' and why? What are we fightin' for?'

Donald Cammell, for one, was in no doubt that the events of Altamont 'actualised' the violent impulse he had attempted to explore through *Performance*.

Altamont happened when we were cutting the film. I remember saying, 'I told you so; you see what rock and roll can do when you get a lot of people into this violent, ritualistic mood.' The ritualistic use of violence was natural to American audiences. It did seem like a re-run of certain aspects of the movie. I felt a little bit prophetic.

He elaborated further in an interview with Anthony Hayden-Guest in 1970, shortly before the film's release:

You have to understand that youth is still attracted
to violence. The Woodstock Nation is attracted to
violence. You can't say to ten million people that
they are all horrified by violence. It's attractive.
Otherwise Mick would not be where he is today.
Mick will probably be annoyed at this. But his
dilemma is that he knows about the violence. This
movie was finished before Altamont and Altamont
actualised it.

In an interview with *Time Out*, two years after the making
of *Performance*, Jagger would offer an intriguing insight into
Cammell's ideas of the relationship between rock music
and violence, and also into his own.

There's two important things about the film to Donald.
There's the sexual thing – not only physically sexual,
but the inter-relating of sexes and the interchanging
of roles. And the role of violence and the role of
women, *vis-à-vis* the role of violence of a man, the
two things can balance each other out. And the
ritualistic significance of violence. That's one of the
main themes if you can gain any conclusion out of
it. Donald's really hung up on the ritual of violence
not being the thing anymore, where certain people
can through certain moods – like a tournament or a
small war – but now that's not being used anymore
that's very dangerous. He's deploring the lack of ritual
in violence. The way of coping with the violence is
to sort of act it out theatrically. I personally don't feel
I have to do it. Part of me does . . .

I don't understand the connection between music and violence. Donald's always trying to explain it to me and I blindly carry on. I just know that I get very aroused by music, but it doesn't arouse me violently. I never went to a rock and roll show and wanted to smash the windows or beat up anybody afterwards. I feel more sexual than physically violent. I get a sexual feeling and I want to fuck as soon as I've been playing. I cool down very quickly. I can come off stage and be back to normal in five minutes. You can only really get into the feeling if you're with a group of people like that. The only time I've felt violent was in some street demonstration and you really get the feeling of being in with a crowd which wants to do something and you get really carried along whether they're right or wrong ... The point is that the act of violence is more powerful than the intellectual political act. I've never felt that feeling in a crowd with music, although I've felt very turned on but not like that.

Jagger would never be as dangerous a figure after Altamont. The sybaritic life became more ostentatious, the narcissism more pronounced. He married Bianca Jagger: his mirror image. At a time when rock stars styled themselves as the new aristocracy, Jagger lorded it over all, part Sun King, part Renaissance bandit.

Unlike Turner, he never succumbed to inertia and ennui; rather Jagger's career has enjoyed an extraordinary longevity, inspired by a robust constitution, his apparently undiminished enthusiasm for performing and his legendary business acumen. He is a man, as he once sang, of wealth and taste, with a fortune estimated to be in excess of £100m, the walls of his five homes hung with Picassos, Renoirs and Van Goghs.

'You're a comical little geezer,' Chas tells Turner in one of the film's immortal lines. 'You'll look funny when you're fifty.' Funny? Mick Jagger's face is so familiar, so iconic, that it is hard to tell whether he looks funny or not. The cheeks more furrowed, the mop of hair improbably intact, the glint in his eye promising one more defiant fling, he just looks like himself.

Johnny Shannon: 'Mick Jagger? A charming fella.'

K

Kray Twins, The

The most notorious criminals in British post-war history, Ronnie and Reggie Kray exercised a mesmerising effect on the public imagination in the 1960s, and were to have a crucial influence on *Performance*. The Krays' organisation and their methods provided an obvious template for Harry Flowers's 'firm', and the character of Flowers himself is clearly modeled on the homosexual Ronnie.

While Donald Cammell never met the Krays personally, he had at least one direct connection to their world in David Litvinoff, who was instrumental in shaping the mood and characterisations for *Performance*. Litvinoff grew up in the East End and fraternised with local villains. A homosexual, he was allegedly once a lover of Ronnie Kray, although that seems unlikely.

The Krays' emergence into popular notoriety owed everything to the dissolution of the traditional class-structure in post-war Britain, and the dawning sense that the working-classes were no longer content to 'know their place' and stay there. The Krays simultaneously embodied a fanciful notion of traditional East End, working-class community and soldiarity – feudal chieftains who, it was said, 'looked after their own' and 'never hurt civilians' – and a glamorous upward mobility. At the height of their

infamy, the Krays consorted with political figures and
show-business celebrities, and received the imprimatur of
entry into 'Swinging London' by being immortalised by
the photographer David Bailey in his book *Goodbye Baby
and Amen*.

They were the first British gangsters seriously to emulate
the example of the American Mafia in their aspirations
to use crime and intimidation as the springboard to 'go
legit', even styling their operation, in a parody of business respectability, as 'the Firm'. Ronnie, in particular,
was infatuated with the legend of Al Capone and the
Chicago gangsters, reading everything he could about
them, copying their dress of discreet, double-breasted
suits and shoulder-padded overcoats and insisting he be
known as 'the Colonel'.

Born in Hoxton, in the East End of London, the
Krays began their career in the 1950s, running crude
protection rackets on pubs, drinking clubs and illegal
bookmakers in their own 'manor', before graduating to
an interest in West End gaming through an association
with the notorious West London slum landlord, Peter
Rachman (see **Powis Square**). When the twins attempted
to extort money from Rachman, he shrewdly steered their
attention to the more profitable pastures of a Knightsbridge
gaming club, Esmeralda's Barn, which the Krays duly
took over. The club was to offer them entry not only
to the lucrative business of providing 'protection' to
other West End clubs, but also to the gilded world of
high-rolling gamblers, show-business stars and the more
raffish elements of London society.

The Krays' emergence into the public eye came via a

story printed in the *Sunday Mirror* in the summer of 1964 under the headline 'Peer and a Gangster: Yard Enquiry', reporting that police were investigating an alleged homosexual relationship between a peer of the realm who was 'a household name' and a 'leading thug' in the London underworld. The peer in question, Lord Boothby, wrote a letter to *The Times*, identifying himself, but denying in detail all the allegations. Five days later the *Daily Mirror* published a full retraction and apology and paid Boothby £40,000 in compensation (the equivalent of £500,000 today).

In fact, the story was substantially true. Boothby was homosexual and Ronnie Kray had been a frequent visitor to his London home; and while there was no evidence that the two men had ever had sexual relations, they did share an interest in tough young men, 'rough trade'.

Ronnie Kray was not named in the original allegation, nor the subsequent apology, but he could not resist the temptation to make capital from it. He supplied the *Daily Express* with a photograph of himself and Boothby seated together in the peer's flat, allaying any remaining doubts that he was the 'leading thug' referred to in the *Mirror*'s allegations. Kray was able to extract an apology from the *Mirror* and, more important, head off the newspaper's enquiries into the Firm's criminal activities. It also made the Krays household names.

They hobnobbed in West End nightclubs, and were photographed with the likes of George Raft and Judy Garland. They developed associations with the American Mafia, 'protecting' their gambling interests in London, and diversified into big business and property fraud. But their ambitions were largely undermined by the psychopathic behaviour of Ronnie. In 1966 he walked into the Blind Beggar public house in East London, drew a 9mm Mauser automatic pistol from his pocket and shot dead George Cornell, a minor gangland figure who was not only associated with the Krays' principal gangland rivals, the Richardsons, but, more significantly, had once slighted Ronnie Kray by calling him 'a fat poof' behind his back. Shortly afterwards, egged on by his brother, Reggie stabbed to death another minor villain, Jack 'The Hat' McVitie. The murders, and the Krays' burgeoning criminal influence, led to a massive investigation by Scotland Yard. They were finally arrested in May 1968 – around the time Donald Cammell was completing his draft of *Performance*.

The preliminary hearing against the Krays opened in July, coinciding with the beginning of the *Performance* shoot. Their trial at the Old Bailey the following year was to prove the longest and most costly to date in British history. The twins were convicted for the murders of Cornell and McVitie. On 8 March 1969, Justice Melford Stevenson sentenced both brothers to life imprisonment with a recommendation that they should serve not less than thirty years. Ronnie Kray had completed almost twenty-eight years of his sentence, the latter part in Broadmoor hospital, when he died of a heart attack in March 1995. Reggie Kray is still imprisoned, and has become a born-again Christian.

L

Laraine

The precocious daughter of Mrs Gibbs, Turner's 'daily'. It is Laraine who ferries tea to Turner, Pherber and Lucy, apparently indifferent to the orgiastic surroundings in which she finds herself. The role was played by Lorraine Wickens, a little girl whom Cammell had come across while he was living in Chelsea, scavenging empty soft-drink bottles in order to collect the refunds. 'She was a little bottle merchant,' he remembered. Her present whereabouts is unknown.

Liars, The

The name of the original film treatment, written by Donald Cammell, on which *Performance* was based. (See *The Performers*.)

Lieberson, Sanford

Producer of *Performance*. Born in Los Angeles of Russian immigrant parents, Lieberson spent two years in the American navy before moving into the entertainment business, following the time-honoured apprenticeship of working in the mail-room at the William Morris agency.

After a spell working in Rome for the Grade Organisation, he returned to Los Angeles and joined Cre-

ative Management Artists (CMA), which numbered Paul
Newman, Barbra Streisand and Judy Garland among its
clients. In 1964 he moved to London to help set up the
London office of CMA, representing Peter Sellers, Richard
Harris and the director Lindsay Anderson among others. He
also represented the Rolling Stones for film and television
work, in which capacity he arranged the group's appearance
in Jean-Luc Godard's *One Plus One*. In 1968, Lieberson left
CMA to set up his own production company, Goodtimes,
for which *Performance* was his first film.

David Puttnam later joined Lieberson as a partner in
Goodtimes, and the pair went on to produce such films
as *Stardust*, *Bugsy Malone*, *The Rolling Stones Rock and Roll
Circus* and *Mahler*. Lieberson later became president of
production for 20th Century Fox and chief of production at Goldcrest films. Most recently, he was head of
production at the National Film and Television School,
and now works as an independent producer.

Litvinoff, David

As dialogue coach and technical adviser on the film,
David Litvinoff was, arguably more than any other single
individual, *Performance*'s guiding and abiding spirit, the
man credited with lending the film its authentic air of
criminality, and also its air of mayhem.

A ubiquitous presence who glided easily between the
worlds of crime and bohemianism, Litvinoff left an indelible mark on all who met him. To Donald Cammell he
was 'quite simply, fantastic'. To the artist Martin Sharp he
was 'in his own way, a genius'. In the words of his friend,

the jazz singer and surrealist George Melly, he was a man who 'understood entirely the excitement of violence'.

The son of a Jewish Russian émigré tailor, Litvinoff was born in Bethnal Green, East London in 1928, one of eight brothers. It was a prodigiously gifted family. One brother, Emmanuel, was to become a novelist; another a historian. David's talents were less specific: he was a mesmeric talker – 'a PhD with honours in street-savvy', according to his friend, the painter Nigel Waymouth; 'the greatest scriptwriter I've ever met', according to Sandy Lieberson, although Litvinoff never wrote a word.

Like a character out of Genet ('Lit was rampantly homosexual,' said Donald Cammell), Litvinoff flitted between the worlds of the artist and the criminal, as mysterious as he was familiar to the habitués of Chelsea's Bohemia, the drinkers in the Colony Room club and those tough East End boys whose overtly macho behaviour disguised other sexual predilections.

Among his friends was the painter Lucian Freud, who executed a drawing of Litvinoff, his head shrouded in a cowl, which Freud entitled *Man in a Headscarf*. It shows a strong, angled face, a prominent Hebraic nose, fleshy lips and downcast eyes.

Christopher Gibbs: 'He was a very puckish character; fortyish, small, but strong and muscular, wearing whatever he'd got hold of.

'He was a great stirrer-upper and an inspired manipulator; his was the gangster East End savvy. He was frightfully thick with Ronnie and Reggie. He was friends with Quentin Crisp. He liked hanging out with these tough boys, Greeks and Italians, mixed with runaway Etonians, spinning thrilling tales to them of this, that and the other. He had a lot of picaresque friends and he liked a good culture clash.'

At various times in his life, Litvinoff worked as a waiter at a Lyons Corner House, as a tipster for the William Hickey column in the *Daily Express* and as a dealer in paintings and second-hand books. But for the most part he seemed to live by his wits.

Christopher Gibbs: 'He never had a job – he didn't believe in being gainfully employed – but knew every likely lad in every pinball arcade. In the best possible way he had not much sense of property. He would go out and just grab a bicycle that happened to be standing nearby. He'd streak up to some shop, go in talking nineteen to the dozen and come out with an enormous cheese and eight loaves of bread without having paid a penny. And then he'd stop in at a bookshop and bring you some book he thought you might be interested in.

'He was a brilliant jester. He used words like a painter using colours he'd never thought of using before. He sometimes spoke in blank verse, accompanied by lots of gestures. It was like an incantation. I loved him very much, but at the same time he was a nightmare to have around.'

David Cammell: 'He just couldn't bear life to be boring. There had to be drama; life was a drama. If it looked remotely like settling down he'd have to disturb it. You never knew what was true and what was invented; it was all a total *mélange*.

'A friend tells a story of how he was looking out of his

window one day and saw David walking past, and called out, "Hi, David." And there was a young policeman nearby, and David immediately called out, "Police officer, arrest this man; he's trying to molest me" ... He was always doing things like that.'

George Melly: 'He loved stirring it up: he loved danger. And he never went to bed, as far as I could see. He lived on Benzedrine.'

To Mick Jagger, Litvinoff was both something of a mentor and a loyal friend. Following the infamous Redlands drug bust in 1967, which resulted in the arrest of Jagger, Keith Richard and the art-dealer Robert Fraser (see **Mars Bars**), a search was launched for the culprit who had 'blown the whistle' to the police. Suspicion settled on a casual acquaintance named Nicky Cramer. Litvinoff visited the unfortunate Cramer and set about beating a confession out of him.

'It was awful, horrible behaviour,' says Christopher Gibbs, who witnessed the incident. Cramer, of course, was innocent.

Deborah Dixon: 'David advised Donald on the London underworld. He knew about everything. He was just a whirlwind coming into the room, six simultaneous conversations on six different levels. His energy and his violence were just incredible, as if his mind didn't fit his body. He could destroy anybody with words.'

Violence shadowed Litvinoff wherever he went.

Christopher Gibbs: There was a very romanticised story which ended up with Litvinoff hanging upside down by his heels somewhere near the Derry and Toms Roof Garden, and waking up with his head shaved, blood streaming down from his wounds into the flowers, hearing the Aldermaston marchers singing 'Corrina, Corrina' as they were coming up Kensington High Street. That was David's version. The truth is that it was something to do with a gambler's debt at Esmeralda's Barn, a gaming room in Knightsbridge.'

An echo of this incident would subsequently find its way into *Performance* in the scene where the barrister's chauffeur is kidnapped in a mews garage by Chas, Rosebloom and Moody; acid is poured over his Rolls-Royce, and the chauffeur's head is shaved by Chas.

Donald Cammell: 'Litvinoff knew how to get people going. I remember he was done up outside a tube station in South London. Straight in the face with a razor blade. It took out the side of his mouth. He showed up at my place in Chelsea. He'd been in a washroom and put a huge band-aid over it, but he was like an animal – he didn't care.

'We took him to hospital, got him stitched up, and he looked terrible. He slept on my floor for two or three days, doped up, and I saw this wound just heal up, as if he'd willed it. And two months later it was just a rather elegant scar. And he looked fabulous.'

It was Litvinoff who arranged for James Fox to visit the Thomas A' Beckett in the Old Kent Road, a boxers' pub, where Fox was introduced to Johnny Shannon, the market-trader and sometime boxing trainer who would tutor him in South London mannerisms, and eventually play the role of Harry Flowers.

Johnny Shannon: 'Coming from the world I came from, David seemed a very strange guy. He rang me one day and asked me to come over to his flat to talk about the film. It was all hurry up all the time. He made me a cup of tea, then we went through the story for two and a half hours and he said, would you like another cup of tea, and he poured it from the same pot. That seemed very strange to me.

'I believe he went to the Bob Dylan concert at the Isle of Wight and broke his arm or leg and just stayed there for two or three days with the break. He was a very weird guy. He knew the [Kray] twins, I think. He used to go around the clubs where the twins were; he'd gamble and get himself in lots of trouble.'

In the 1970s Litvinoff retreated to Wales. 'I think he felt he had to,' says George Melly. 'There was probably some trouble, but I don't remember what it was. He didn't much like the countryside. He couldn't bear the fact that there was all that grass and no-one was doing anything with it. He referred to all birds as sparrows, whether they were eagles or robins or whatever they were.'

From Wales he moved to Australia.

Nigel Waymouth: 'David was very, very lazy. Someone gave him an advance for a screenplay for a movie, and he just took off for seven months. He had an idea for a musical based on the life of Anthony Armstrong Jones [Lord Snowdon], called *Tony*. But he never wrote it, of course.'

He returned to England, homeless and penniless. His old friend Christopher Gibbs came to his rescue, inviting him to stay at Davington Priory, his home in Faversham, Kent.

Christopher Gibbs: 'He grew older and tireder – not a condition that agreed with him.

'He wasn't an ace listener, and he was quite an exhausting person to have around. After he'd been staying for three and a half years I said he had to find somewhere else to live. I went to Scotland and while I was gone he gave away all my clothes. He was a very generous man.

'And then he killed himself, with an overdose of sleeping pills. He left me a note which I found three months later, hidden in some shirts. He'd go through my drawers all the time; you'd find him examining the stubs in your chequebook, complaining about how much you were spending on suits or in Italian restaurants. He loved blues music. His note said: "I've made eight tapes for you in such and such a box; please send another tape marked X to somebody in Australia." No question of "I'm terribly sorry to have been such a nuisance", or anything like that.'

Nigel Waymouth: 'Two days before he killed himself, my son went down to Kent to visit him. David told him he was going away on a long journey and might not be coming back. Three years earlier he'd told me he planned to commit suicide. He said he couldn't face old age. He couldn't even face middle age.'

Christopher Gibbs: 'His brothers were horrified. How could he do this in the house of a *goyim*! We had a Jewish funeral out on the Essex marshes.'

Gibbs later sold Davington Priory to Bob Geldof. It was where Geldof planned Live Aid.

Lowndes Square

While the exterior shots of Turner's house were done in Powis Square (though at number 25 rather than 81), most of the interiors were shot at 15 Lowndes Square, Knightsbridge, a house owned by Captain Leonard Plugge.

Plugge was a colourful and eccentric ornament to British public life: a politician, inventor, scientist, gambler, party-goer and art collector. As the Conservative member of parliament for Chatham, in Kent, in the 1930s, he would make excursions to his constituency in a twin-funnelled motor yacht which he kept moored on the Thames opposite the House of Commons.

An expert ice-skater, he distinguished himself during the war by raising questions in the House on such varied issues as the use of lipstick in the armed forces, and the possibilities of delivering mail by rocket. He subsequently invented the first car-radio, which he installed in his large American car, claiming he could make contact with some-one armed with a similar device up to thirty miles away.

The Lowndes Square house – the sole remaining private residence in a square where all the other houses had been turned into flats – was empty at the time of filming *Performance*, Plugge having installed himself in a flat in nearby Dolphin Square.

The rental of the house was arranged by David Cammell, although by coincidence Plugge's son had been the best friend at Eton of Christopher Gibbs, who was responsible for styling the interiors for Performance. 'We were both sacked, for running a gang of shoplifters,' says Gibbs.

David Cammell: 'The house had been used as a private gambling school, which is how I'd heard of it. Donald originally wanted to install the cast in the house and have them live there for a month or two. In the end, we rented it on the condition that Plugge's art-collection, which was still hanging on the walls, should be insured for £1m.

'It was a very intense, very peculiar situation. After we'd moved in we discovered that there was a mongol living at the top of the house, with lice-infested blankets and an Alsatian dog. He stayed there throughout the shoot. And every so often Captain Plugge would arrive in a beaver-lined coat, supported by a changing cast of exotic young girls.

'Halfway through we got a lawyer's letter from the next-door neighbours, complaining about the catering vans parked outside. They took us to court. Plugge's solicitor was a hunch-backed dwarf. In the end we had to pay for the neighbours to go away on a holiday.'

Captain Plugge later retired to Beverly Hills. Meanwhile, his daughter, Gale-Ann Benson, became embroiled with an American Black Power leader named Hakim Jamal, after meeting him at the home of the actor and SWP member Corin Redgrave. In 1971, after changing her name to Hale Kimba, she followed Jamal to Trinidad, where they joined Michael X, the self-styled Black Power leader and former enforcer for the slum landlord Peter Rachman (see **Powis Square**). In 1972, her body was found in a shallow grave. She had been hacked to death by a machete. Michael X was found guilty of plotting her murder. In 1974 he was executed for the murder of a barber, Joseph Skerritt, and hanged. Benson's murderer, Stanley Abbott, was also hanged.

Lucy

The young French girl, played by Michèle Breton, who lives with Turner and Pherber in Turner's Powis Square home.

In his treatment 'The Performers', Cammell offers a concise definition of her character and type. 'Lucy is Pherber at seventeen.'

Just as Pherber was Anita Pallenberg playing herself, there is ample evidence to suggest that Lucy was a mirror-image of Michèle Breton: the free-spirited hippie-chick, open to whatever experience presents itself, simultaneously innocent and old beyond her years.

What on earth is she doing there? Breton was 'found' by Donald Cammell on the beach at St Tropez and taken to Paris, where she lived in a *ménage à trois* with Cammell and Deborah Dixon. We do not know where Lucy has come from, but we can imagine some similarities with Breton's own circumstances; like Cammell and Dixon, Turner and Pherber are not simply Lucy's lovers, but her mentors, her sojourn in Powis Square an opportunity to further her education in life. That, at least, is what she has suggested to the immigration authorities: she is in 'a place of learning' where Pherber 'is learning me English and my boyfriend is learning me History and Magic and books and stuff'.

Lucy is the androgynous 'girl-boy' type that Cammell himself supposedly had a particular liking for; in *Performance* she is a powerful cipher for his exploration of the blurring of sexual identity. When we first see her, in bed with Turner, in a tangle of limbs and hair, we cannot be sure whether she is male or female (nor indeed, whether *he* is male or female). Her subsequent encounter with Chas, his attraction to her androgynous physique – 'You're a skinny little frog, aren't you . . . small titties, haven't you, you're like a small boy, that's what you're like . . .' – is a measure of how far he has travelled in his mind under the ministrations of Turner and Pherber. The tenderness of their encounter is in vivid contrast to the violent, solipsistic encounter with his girlfriend Dana at the beginning of the film.

What does Lucy see in Chas? Clearly, he embodies her romantic fascination with danger – the type of danger which intrigues and excites her as she ponders the pictures of the mountains of Persia with Turner. Would the mountains be more beautiful without the bandits? '*Je ne sais pas* . . .'

We can speculate that, like Michèle Breton, Lucy travels East in search of her dream. There her consumption of copious amounts of hashish is soon supplemented with heroin. Her passport and belongings are stolen or sold. In a mountain village, or perhaps a cheap tourist hotel, Lucy dies of an overdose. Or she finds her way to India, the

Maharishi's ashram at Rishikesh, or a Tibetan monastery in Nepal, where she forswears the ephemeral revelations of drugs for God. Eventually she returns to France, marries an academic and writes an autobiography in which the death of Turner is but a footnote.

M

Mad Cyril

The unseen 'heavy' who Rosebloom suggests should help turn over Joey Maddocks's betting-shop.

> *Flowers*: I want that shop redecorated tomorrow night, straight after closing time. Four handed's enough ... The Brown Boys ... They like a laugh.
> *Rosebloom*: And Mad Cyril?
> *Chas*: What?
> *Flowers*: Why not? Pop in ... pop out ... You know what I mean. Be ... placatory. I like that. Turn it up ...

Mad Cyril is also mentioned in the 'Memo From Turner' sequence.

He was later memorialised in a song of the same name by the Manchester rock band the Happy Mondays.

Magritte, René (1898–1967)

Belgian surrealist painter, one of whose paintings is bought to Turner's Powis Square mansion by two art-dealers (played by the Myers twins) for his perusal. Nic Roeg felt it was important for the scene that the painting should be authentic, not a print. George Melly, the jazz singer and surrealist, and a friend of David Litvinoff, was approached to see if he would loan a Magritte from his own collection. Melly, not surprisingly, declined. In a conversation with Victor Bockris some years later, Roeg talked of his arguments with Warner over providing a painting.

> I was determined to get [an authentic Magritte]. So we talked to the studio and the studio said, 'Oh, that's quite ridiculous.' And I said, 'We can rent one from a gallery, I know what gallery we can rent it from.' And the guy said, 'Are you crazy? You can get a print. Rent a Magritte! That's really . . . you don't know what you're doing.' I said, fuck it, I am going to get it on that set. We are going to have a real thing. We don't want a photograph or print. So all right, if they won't get it we'll rent it ourselves. We rented it. When the painting came on the set it changed the atmosphere of the set. And Mick had a look . . . because the print wouldn't have done it. It was behind him. He takes down a fake painting and puts up the Magritte. Even the prop man was . . . 'Cor, £40,000.' It created a tension. I mean, Mick was performing in front of it and it gave it a different tone . . .

In the end, Turner refuses to buy the painting, because 'It's too expensive'. But he does buy the frame. It is last seen framing his blood-stained body in the basement cupboard.

Mars Bars

On the run from Harry Flowers, Chas arrives at the Powis Square house of Turner. On the doorstep is that morning's delivery of milk, and two Mars bars. Something to help Turner work, rest and play?

A caramel and chocolate confection manufactured by the Mars confectionery company, the Mars bar became a peculiar object of folklore in Britain in 1967, following a notorious police raid on Redlands, the Sussex home of Rolling Stone Keith Richard.

By 1967, the Stones' reputation as youthful rebels and enemies of the establishment was in the ascendant, making them a target for public moralists and the British press. In January of that year the group released the single 'Let's Spend The Night Together', prompting an energetic debate in the press about their corrosive effect on public morals. Their refusal in the same month to take part in the much-loved ritual of waving goodbye from the revolving stage on the television variety programme *Sunday Night at the London Palladium* simply compounded the felony.

Early in February, Britain's most scurrilous muck-raking newspaper, the *News of the World*, ran a story alleging that LSD parties had been held at a house in south-west London belonging to the group the Moody Blues. Of more interest to the *News of the World* was the allegation that Mick Jagger had also visited the house.

Determined to nail their man, the newspaper published

an article two weeks later claiming that Jagger had been seen at Blaises night-club in Kensington taking Benzedrine tablets and showing a lump of hash to two girls and inviting them to his flat 'for a smoke'. Alas for the *News of the World*, in the murky shadows of the night-club the paper had confused Jagger with Brian Jones.

That same evening, Jagger appeared on television on the *Eamonn Andrews Show* denying the story and announcing that he intended to issue a writ for libel.

A routine dirt-digging enquiry into rock-star morals now became a vendetta.

The following weekend, Jagger and Marianne Faithful joined a house-party at Keith Richard's country home. Also in the party were Christopher Gibbs, Robert Fraser, Michael Cooper and George and Patti Harrison. The most welcome guest was David Schneidermann, an American known as 'the Acid King', who had procured supplies of the legendary Owsley's Sunshine LSD for the weekend. Two others were present, Robert Fraser's Moroccan aide-de-camp, Ali, and a hippie acquaintance of Richard's named Nicky Cramer.

Sunday was spent in a leisurely stoned ramble around the lanes and beaches of West Sussex (recorded for posterity in some particularly evocative photographs by Cooper) before the party returned to Redlands for an evening's relaxation. The Harrisons departed, leaving the others to settle down in front of the television. Marianne Faithfull, having taken a bath, had wrapped herself in a large fur rug. That was the utterly domestic and wholly innocent scene which confronted the police when they raided the premises late on Sunday evening.

They seized some amphetamine tablets, which Marianne Faithfull had slipped into Mick Jagger's pocket on a recent visit to France, and heroin belonging to Robert Fraser (overlooking, astonishingly, Schneidermann's cache of LSD).

The following Sunday, the raid was reported in some detail in the *News of the World*, omitting names, but raising suspicions that the newspaper had tipped off the police in the first place. It was a search for a possible informant that led to the beating of the unfortunate Nicky Cramer (see **David Litvinoff**).

The ensuing trial became a national *cause célèbre*. There was an outcry when, pending sentence, both Jagger and Fraser were taken from the court in handcuffs to spend a night in Lewes jail. The following day, the court was regaled with accounts of the police raid, including details of 'the young lady on the settee', wearing only a 'light-coloured fur rug which, from to time, she allowed to fall, disclosing her nude body'. Although not mentioned by name, there was no doubt in anybody's mind that the young woman in question was Marianne Faithfull. The lurid image conjured up of a den of drugs and depravity with the wanton Faithfull, the sole woman among eight men, wrapped only in a rug, immediately elevated her to the dubious national status of Scarlet Woman. It also gave rise to a bizarre and salacious rumour that, within days of the trial, would sweep across Britain. This held that when the police burst into the house they had interrupted Mick Jagger in the act of licking a Mars bar inserted into Faithfull's vagina. The story was a complete fabrication, but would quickly assume the status of folklore. Faithfull would later recount that the first she knew of it was when Jagger told her he had heard it from a prisoner in Wormwood Scrubs, where he was being held on remand. It was, she remarked, simply 'a dirty old man's fantasy'.

At the conclusion of the trial, Keith Richard was sentenced to prison for one year for allowing his house to be used for the smoking of cannabis. Robert Fraser was sentenced to six months for possession of heroin, and Jagger sentenced to three months for possession of amphetamines.

The severity of the sentences provoked a public outcry. There were demonstrations in Piccadilly Circus, and outside the *News of the World* offices in Bouverie St (the paper subsequently admitted that it had tipped off the police about the house party, claiming that the information had come from a reader). But the most surprising response came from William Rees-Mogg, the editor of *The Times*, who published the celebrated editorial, entitled (after William Blake) 'Who Breaks a Butterfly on a Wheel?', which argued that Jagger's sentence was cruelly inappropriate – a reflection not of the severity of his offence, but of his notoriety.

The sentence and conviction against Keith Richard were subsequently quashed on appeal. Jagger's conviction was upheld, but his prison sentence was quashed and a one-year conditional discharge imposed in its place. Robert Fraser's appeal was dismissed, and with remission he served four months of his six-month sentence. And Marianne Faithfull would be plagued by mentions of Mars bars evermore.

Mazzola, Frank

Editor on the final cut of *Performance* (see **The Edit**).

Born in Los Angeles, the child of vaudeville actors, Frank Mazzola was Hollywood through and through. As a student at Hollywood High, and sometime teenage gang-member, Mazzola was recruited by the director Nicholas Ray in the early fifties to tutor James Dean in gangland mores for Dean's first film, *Rebel Without a Cause*. Mazzola also had a part in the film as one of Dean's sidekicks. From acting, Mazzola moved to editing, working on innumerable Hollywood films before meeting Donald Cammell and working on *Performance*.

He subsequently worked with Cammell as editor of *Demon Seed* (1977) and on the original cut of *Wild Side*. In 1998 Mazzola completed work on the last, unseen film of Donald Cammell.

On arriving in California, Cammell's first project, following the completion of *Performance*, was to be a film entitled *Ishtar*. The project was aborted, but not before Cammell had shot some preliminary, experimental footage in the Mojave desert of an argument between a film director and a goddess named Aisha (played by Myriam Gibril). The footage ended up stored, and forgotten, in the garage of Frank Mazzola's house, only to be discovered by him shortly after Cammell's death. Redubbed and edited, the film, entitled *The Argument*, has since been screened at festivals in America and Europe.

Meadows, Stanley

English character actor who played the role of Rosebloom.

Ironically, before *Performance* Meadows's film roles had tended to cast him in the role of policeman rather than villain – a case, perhaps, of Cammell wilfully casting against type.

'Donald and Nic took one look at me,' Meadows told *Neon* magazine, 'and both said, "That's the face we want."'

'Memo From Turner'

His mind rearranged by the combination of fly agaric and Pherber's sexual games, Chas follows Turner to his music-room. There Turner, his demon restored, taunts Chas, gyrating with a rod of shimmering neon (to the incantatory strains of Ry Cooder and Merry Clayton's performance of 'Hound Dog'), until Chas himself catches the rhythm and spirals into a full-blown hallucination. Through his eyes we are transported back to Harry Flowers's office, but the figure in the chair is not Flowers but Turner, in a shark-skin suit, hair slicked back, issuing instructions as his henchman dance attendance. Here the figure of the rock star and the gangster are fused for the first time in Chas's imagination, an intimation of *Performances*'s closing moments.

Jagger's performance is a striking cameo of sadistic power. His leer has never seemed more malevolent than in the role of Turner/Flowers, tauntingly exposing the latent homosexuality within the gangster's strutting machismo. 'Let's have a look – take 'em off!' he barks, as the mood of the song becomes increasingly orgiastic, and the gang comply with varying degrees of enthusiasm and reluctance, the final freeze-frame of their naked bodies entwined on the floor equally suggestive of a violent massacre or post-coital exhaustion.

The song itself caused untold problems. Cammell originally hoped that the Stones' songwriting team of Jagger and Keith Richard would write it. But Richard's disapproval of Jagger being involved in the film in the first place, and his rising anxiety and anger about Jagger's relationship with Anita Pallenberg, sabotaged the plan.

In his book *The Stones*, Philip Norman writes that eventually Cammell himself sat down to write 'Memo From Turner', but when the Stones assembled in the studio to record the song it sounded 'still and lifeless'. In the end, Norman writes, Cammell had to badger Jagger into completing the project. 'I took him into a pub in Berwick Street,' said Cammell, 'and said, "Mick, for God's sake, what about the song." Standing there at the bar, he suddenly burst into tears. It was a thing he could always do for maximum effect – just like John Gielgud. "I'm sorry," he said. "I blew it." It was then that I realised he'd decided to get the song finished. From then on, after all that indecisiveness, the decisions were made like *lightning*.'

'Memo From Turner' was re-recorded with a session group, including Steve Winwood and Jim Capaldi from Traffic.

Moody

Member of Harry Flowers's gang, played by John Bindon. Moody is the archetypal slab of hired muscle, a man who does as he's told and doesn't ask questions, whose first loyalty is to his own survival – a man who enjoys his work. As he puts it, preparing to shave the head of Harley-Brown's chauffeur: 'Violence is my game, violence pure and simple.'

Our first glimpse of Moody, chauffeuring Chas through the London streets, gives us a glimpse of the trenchant, xenophobic moralist. He laments the violence in a television programme he has been watching the previous evening, shown at a time with 'kiddies still viewing. Geezer with his ear half hanging off ... I mean, it's not right, Chas. How they going to grow up ...?' He interrupts to tear a strip off another driver – 'Bastard foreign female!' – and then methodically goes about his business of wrecking a mini-cab office and terrorising its employees.

Moody's loyalty blows like a flag in the wind. Although notionally Chas's henchman, when Chas goes on the run after murdering Joey Maddocks it is Moody, egged on by the saturnine Dennis, who spells out exactly what measures need to be taken.

> *Dennis*: Moody ...
> *Moody*: What?
> *Dennis*: What would you do, Moody?
> *Moody*: Eh?
> *Dennis*: With a mad dog, Moody ... where the poor animal is liable to bite you ...
> *Moody*: Bite me?
> *Dennis*: Without meaning to.
> *Moody*: Put it to sleep, Dennis.

Moody's feral instincts are displayed later in the film, when he and Rosebloom visit Chas's friend Tony, trying to establish Chas's whereabouts. While Tony talks to Chas on the phone, Moody eyes up Tony's wife, lying in bed, rigid with fear, in a Terylene night-gown. The look on Moody's face says it all. Never mind the terror, in the parlance of Moody's world, ''E'd give her one . . .'

Morton, Anthony

British actor who plays Dennis, one of Harry Flowers's gang. Anthony Morton would later reach a far wider audience than his part in *Performance* ever granted him by landing a long-running role as a chef in the television soap-opera *Crossroads*.

Myers Twins, The

Identical twin brothers who make a cameo appearance, delivering to Powis Square the Magritte painting which Turner eventually declines to buy. The Myers twins were a ubiquitous adornment of the London party and fashion scene of the time. Their present whereabouts is unknown.

N

Naked Gangsters, The

Johnny Shannon: 'Donald was a very crafty guy. You'd go through the script and do something, and next day he'd put his arm around your shoulder and say, "I think we could do this . . ." My contract had finished and they rang to say they wanted to do another scene. When the driver came I said, what suit have I got to wear, and he kept his head down . . . Well, what it was, they'd decided they were doing this nude scene with Harry Flowers and his gang. I just fell about laughing; I couldn't imagine myself doing it.

'Tony Morton didn't want to do it, so Donald took him out for lunch; they had a couple of bottles of wine, and there was Tony suggesting better ways to do it. Johnny Bindon loved it. He wanted to get undressed before anybody else, but he had quite a lot to boast about, of course. He was most upset they only wanted a back view.'

Stanley Meadows [quoted in *Neon* magazine]: 'Donald wanted me to take my clothes off – one of his last-minute inspirations! I said no. He said, "What if Fellini asked you to do it?" I said, "You're not Fellini." Fortunately my contract stipulated I was not to display my genitals.'

Nitzsche, Jack

Soundtrack co-ordinator for *Performance* (see **The Soundtrack**).

A legendary figure in the rock world, with a career spanning almost forty years, Nitzsche has worked as a composer/arranger/producer for everybody from Phil Spector and Tim Buckley to Doris Day and the Byrds. In recent years he has been one of Hollywood's most industrious and successful composers of film soundtracks.

Born in 1937 in Chicago, Nitzsche's first job in the record industry was working for Art Rupe's Specialty Records in the early sixties, writing lead sheets for the label's A&R director, Sonny Bono. Through Bono he was introduced to Phil Spector, going on to work as an arranger on many of Spector's 'wall of sound' hits.

Nitzsche first became acquainted with the Rolling Stones in 1964 (when the group recorded at the RCA studios in Hollywood), playing keyboards and percussion on some songs and later arranging the choir on 'You Can't Always Get What You Want'.

His work on *Performance* was the prelude to an illustrious career in film. He has scored and supervised the music for more than two dozen films including *One Flew Over the Cuckoo's Nest*, *Blue Collar*, *The Jewel of the Nile*, *9½ Weeks* and *The Crossing Guard*. In 1982 he received an Oscar for 'Up Where We Belong', a song he co-wrote with Will Jennings and Buffy Sainte-Marie for the film *An Officer and a Gentleman*.

In an interview with Harvey Kubernick in the Los Angeles *New Times*, Nitzsche recalled that *Performance* 'is the only movie I have ever done where nobody interfered. Nobody. Donald Cammell would drop by the studio once in a while. He let me do whatever I wanted. I put all kinds of weird shit in that score. It was amazing. And Anita on the screen. God damm ... To this day, I'll be in a restaurant, or walking down a street or leaving a screening on a lot, somewhere like at Paramount, and someone will yell out *Performance!* Recently, Billy Friedkin saw me walking across the street and yelled, "*Performance!* The greatest use of music in a motion picture ever!"'

Noel

The musician who is the original tenant of Turner's basement flat. It is overhearing Noel's conversation with his 'mum' at Paddington station about the vacant flat which steers Chas to Powis Square. The part of Noel was played by Noel Swabey. 'Mum' was played by Helen Booth.

O

Old Man of the Mountain, The

'Nothing is true,' Turner tells Chas, as the effects of the fly agaric mushroom take hold. 'Everything is permitted.'

Chas is confused. 'Eh?'

> *Turner*: Last words of Hassan-I-Sabbah. The Old Man of the Mountain.
> *Pherber*: His motto . . . It's a thousand years old. Imagine yourself a thousand years younger . . .

It might also be the motto of *Performance*: 'Nothing is true. Everything is permitted.' As a declaration of moral freedom, the last words of Hassan-I-Sabbah parallel Aleister Crowley's dictum: 'Do what thou wilt shall be the whole of the law.' In other words, the society of men is shaped by the laws and conventions of man's own making, which are provisional and illusory. True morality is not a matter of social convention but of self-knowledge. As Bob Dylan put it, 'to live outside the law you must be honest'.

(Another Dylan line comes to mind to describe Chas's predicament: 'You know something's happening, but you don't know what it is . . . do you . . . ?')

al-Hassan ibn-al-Sabbah (to give him his correct name) was the leader of a fanatical Persian sect known as the

Ismalians, who in the twelfth century waged a reign of terror from their fortress at Alamut, high in the mountains south of the Caspian Sea, earning al-Hassan notoriety among the Crusaders as 'the old man of the mountain'.

The Ismalians were organised into an elaborate hierarchy. Below the grand master stood the grand priors – the equivalent of regional chieftains; below them were the propagandists for the movement, and finally there were the '*fida'is*', or foot-soldiers, who carried out assassinations on the grand master's orders.

The most colourful, and oft-quoted, account of the Ismalians' activities was provided by Marco Polo, who passed through Alamut in 1271 or 1272 – some 150 years after al-Hassan's death. *The Adventures of Marco Polo* describes the magnificent gardens which al-Hassan constructed around his palace at Alamut, and the method by which he would prepare his 'self-sacrificing ones' for their murderous tasks.

Now no man was allowed to enter the Garden save those whom he intended to be his Ashishin. There was a fortress at the entrance to the Garden, strong enough to resist all the world, and there was no other way to get in. He kept at his court a number of the youths of the country, from twelve to twenty years of age, such as had a taste for soldiering ... Then he would introduce them into his Garden, some four, six or ten at a time, having first made them drink a certain potion which cast them into a deep sleep, and then causing them to be lifted and carried in. So

when they awoke they found themselves in the
Garden.

When therefore they awoke, and found themselves in a place so charming, they deemed that it was
Paradise in very truth. And the ladies and damsels
dallied with them to their heart's content . . .

It is an abbreviated version of this story which Turner
reads as Pherber ritualistically dresses Chas in a sumptuous
silk kaftan, powders his body and face, and hands him a
dagger which Chas tucks into his sash. Pherber pulls back
the top of the kaftan and anoints Chas with a kiss to his
chest, as Turner reads on.

Thus it was that when the Old Man decided to send
one of his assassins upon a mission such as to have a
Prince slain, he would say to one of these youths,
'Go and kill and when thou returnest my Angels
shall bear thee into Paradise.'

The implication is clear. In reading the account Turner
is not only making a connection between the twelfth-
century assassins and Chas. Through his awakening to the
sensual, Chas has been gifted with a glimpse of Paradise in
preparation for his next act of assassination – killing Turner
himself.

Turner continues reading. 'And should'st thou die,
nevertheless will I send my Angels to carry thee back
into Paradise.' He looks up from the book. 'They enjoyed
their work.'

Pherber turns to Chas and asks him, 'Are you in that Garden?'

> *Chas*: Yeah!
> *Pherber*: Never trust old men – old show men – old wankers . . .

Central to the legend of the Old Man of the Mountain is the suggestion that the potion with which al-Hassan would drug his young murderers was hashish, giving rise to the belief that the word 'assassin' derives from the Arabic word *haschisin*, meaning hashish-user.

In his book *The Assassin Legends: Myths of the Isma'ilis*, Farhad Daftary argues that the attribution of the epithet 'hashish eaters' or 'hashish takers' is a misnomer derived from the enemies of the Isma'ilis, and is not mentioned in any Muslim sources. A more likely explanation, according to Daftary, is that the word 'assassin' is a corruption of the term for the followers of al-Hassan – *Hassassin*.

Persia resurfaces later in *Performance* as a mythical place of escape. Lounging on the bed, Lucy asks Turner why Chas is planning to go to America. 'I dunno,' says Turner. 'It's the place for a gangster, I guess.' Lucy is looking through an antique card-viewer at a vividly coloured landscape of deserts and mountains. 'I think he should go there . . . Look, the mountains of Persia.'

'Yeah,' says Turner. 'Maybe you're right.'

'I'm sure there's some bandits over there. Don't you think?'

Turner thinks on this and turns to leave. 'Tell me

something,' he asks. 'Do you think the mountains would be improved without the bandits?'

'*Je sais pas,*' says Lucy.

Later, in bed with Chas, she returns to the subject of Persia, telling him that 'I wishes you'd be a bandit in Persia.' When, finally, he leaves to meet his fate, he scrawls a note for Lucy which we see Rosebloom place on the table. 'Gone to Persia.'

P

Pallenberg, Anita (b. 1942)

Seductive and disturbing. Breathtakingly beautiful. Clever, ambitious and manipulative. A hedonistic adventuress. A sharp-tongued temptress, a caster of spells. Are we describing Anita Pallenberg or Pherber, the role she plays in *Performance*?

Swiss by ancestry but raised in Rome, the daughter of a 'frustrated composer' who owned a travel agency, Anita Pallenberg grew up in a cosmopolitan and artistic atmosphere. As a teenager she studied picture restoration and graphic design before an affair with the Italian painter Mario Schifano took her to New York. There she fraternised with the painters Larry Rivers and Andy Warhol and briefly worked as an assistant to Jasper Johns. She also developed a nascent career as a fashion-model, which was to bring her back to Europe, where she threw herself energetically into the fashion and party scene.

Pallenberg entered the Rolling Stones' circle in 1965, when she insinuated herself backstage at a concert in Munich. 'I offered them some hash,' she later recalled. 'They were shocked. They said, "Oh no. We can't smoke before we go on stage." But I started to talk with Brian. He seemed the most open-minded.' They spent that night together, and shortly afterwards Pallenberg moved into Jones's London home.

Pallenberg had become friends with Robert Fraser and Christopher Gibbs through her affair with Mario Schifano; now she in turn introduced Jones to that circle. Gibbs would later remember her as 'absolutely electrifying. Whenever she came into a room, every head would turn to look at her.'

Pallenberg's relationship with Jones was an immediate cause of unease within the tightly knit circle of the Stones. She was someone who took what she wanted. She had a sharp way of needling people, putting them down. She claimed to be a witch, and nobody was sure if she was joking. Mick Jagger, allegedly, was particularly wary of her and her potentially disruptive presence and told his girlfriend at the time, Chrissie Shrimpton, that she was to have nothing to do with her. But despite Jagger's disapproval, Pallenberg and Jones became inseparable.

Their relationship was ever eventful. Accounts of the day talk of frantic sexual sessions between the two, sometimes using whips. When *Stern* magazine wanted to photograph Jones for a cover-story, it was Pallenberg who suggested that he should dress up in the uniform of a Nazi SS officer and pose crushing a doll under his jackbooted heel. The pictures were never used, but the session caused an outcry in the British press. Pallenberg confessed that it 'was all my idea. It was naughty, but what the hell . . . He looked good in SS uniform.'

The two seemed to bring out the worst in each other. In Philip Norman's book *The Stones*, Christopher Gibbs recalled a trip to Morocco in the summer of 1966, dominated by strife and argument. 'They fought about everything – cars, prices, restaurant menus. Brian could never win an argument with Anita although he always made the mistake of trying. There would be terrible scenes with both of them screaming at each other. The difference was that Brian didn't know what he was doing. Anita did know what she was doing. I think that in a more gracious age, Anita would have been called a witch.'

It was on another trip to Morocco the following year, in the immediate aftermath of the Redlands bust, that Anita finally transferred her affections from Jones to Keith Richard – a fact which plunged Jones into depression and exacerbated his growing estrangement from the rest of the band.

Shortly afterwards, Pallenberg moved into Redlands, living in singular domesticity with Richard and his giant deer-hound, Syphilis. By this time, Pallenberg had begun to develop a modest film career, appearing in two films directed by her friend Volker Schlöndorff, and in Roger Vadim's *Barbarella*.

Sandy Lieberson: 'Donald wanted Anita in *Performance*. He'd seen her in Schlöndorff's *A Degree of Murder*. She was wonderful in that film, quite extraordinary, an amazing-looking woman, and Donald thought it would hot things up with Mick to have her in our film. Mick liked the idea – he'd seen her on the screen and thought, "OK, she's an actress, plus we hang out together and she's part of the group." He felt comfortable with her, in bed, around, all that sort of thing. It was a convivial atmosphere.'

*   *   *

Anita Pallenberg: 'I knew Donald and Deborah, so I knew the script of *Performance* long before I was offered the part. I remember once in St Tropez, on the beach, Donald had the script and the wind blew all the pages into the sea. We had to take it back and iron it.

'But I wasn't even supposed to do *Performance*. Tuesday Weld was the actress they wanted to use. She came to England. Then one night she broke her arm; there was some horseplay going on. So that's how I got the role. I had an abortion to do the film, so I was really upset. So that was a bad start already for me.'

The art-dealer Robert Fraser rented Pallenberg his flat at 23 Mount Street in Mayfair for the duration of the shoot, 'and then he never moved out, so all he rented me was the bed'.

Pallenberg recalled that she was paid £25,000 for the role. 'It was ridiculous. I was like a baby. I didn't have a brain, didn't know how to look after myself.

'Performance was about what was going on at the time – the kind of attitudes; relaxed, cool, groovy. The *ménage à trois*, the dressing up. But what I remember most is just sitting around for hours and hours waiting for Nic Roeg. It was the most tedious thing I've ever done.'

It was during the making of *Performance* that Pallenberg started using heroin in earnest, supplied to her on surreptitious visits to the set by her dealer 'Spanish Tony' Sanchez (see **The Shoot**). 'After the film, I was pregnant with [her first child] Marlon. We went off to South America with Mick and Marianne. Then Brian died. The Stones did Altamont. Then we went to the South of France and did *Exile on Main Street*, and the drugs got worse. So I think *Performance* was the end of the beautiful Sixties – love and all that. That film marked the end for me. I can't even remember the film coming out. I'd forgotten about it completely.'

For the next ten years, Pallenberg was enveloped in drug addiction. At the end of the Seventies she separated from Keith Richard and after two sojourns in treatment centres finally conquered her addiction. 'It was like taking a big plunge over a cliff. Very scary. I had to find out how to go out shopping. I couldn't even do that, I was too scared, too paranoid. Because with the Stones we had all these runners around who'd pick us up and carry us everywhere; sometimes even carry us downstairs, put us in a limousine and on to the aeroplane – for many years. So it was actually the most difficult thing in my life.'

After taking a course in fashion design, Pallenberg worked with the English designer Vivienne Westwood. She is now writing her autobiography.

Performance, Life is Just a

Talking to a BBC film crew, some thirty years after *Performance* was made, Donald Cammell would describe one of the principal themes of the film as 'a revolution in perception – the interchangeability of gender, and the possibility that human personality was interchangeable on a level that we aren't really aware of yet. That we can inhabit each other's minds at certain stages, and to such an extent that . . . you actually become somebody else.'

In Borgesian terms, 'every man is two men', and conversely two men may become one.

Both Chas and Turner are performers, imprisoned in their respective roles and seeking, with varying degrees of self-awareness, some way to break free of them.

The faces we choose to show to the world at any given time are merely masks, shaped by conditioning and personal choice. Chas is trapped in his role by the strictures of the 'straight world' of the criminal underclass that he moves in and which demands that he act out an ideal of masculinity which denies his latent sexuality. Violence is his life-raft, expressed in his subconscious hatred of women, his suspicion of foreigners, of any sort of otherness; it is his defence against any recognition of the true nature of himself.

Of course, self-reflection would be anathema to a man like Chas. He has no awareness that his life is a performance in the metaphorical sense, although his apparently spontaneous choice of disguise – as a night-club juggler – is, perhaps, as much an unconscious allusion to this as it is a clumsy attempt to secure a foothold in the Turner household.

'A *jongleur*, eh?' says Turner. 'A performer of natural magic . . .'
Chas: Well, I perform.
Turner: I'll bet you do sir, I can tell by your . . . your . . . vibrations.

Turner's performance is, on the face of it, the more obvious one. He is a rock star, after all, a man whose existence is defined in those moments when he is on stage, whose power depends on his ability to manipulate an audience, to project an idealised version of their dreams and desires. Having lost this power – his demon – and mindful that he can no longer conjure the magic he once did, he has become a husk; a man stranded and bemused, who has retreated from the public truth of his failure and insulated himself in a private world of narcissistic distractions.

Everything about Turner suggests a man whose life is an act. He masks himself in the make-up of the artiste (applied by his willing accomplice Pherber); his figure-hugging leotard and slippers suggest a tight-rope walker, the juggler which Chas claims to be – or a jester. He makes magic with mirrors and knives. His life has lost its purpose.

Each man functions as a distorted mirror of what the other either suppresses or desires. For Chas, Turner is what he has never had but what may save him. For Turner, Chas embodies what he has lost and hopes to regain.

Turner's motive in dismantling Chas is to discover what is missing in himself. 'He wants to know,' Pherber tells Chas, 'why your show is a bigger turn-on than his ever was.'

'How would I know?' says Chas. 'But I know a thing or two about the clientele, believe me, boy – they're a bunch of liars and wrigglers. Put the frighteners on 'em. A bit of stick. That's the way to make 'em jump. They love it.'

Sexually, too, each contains what the other needs. Chas denies the female aspect of his sexuality through displays of crude machismo. Turner's masculinity is suffocated by the feminine cocoon he wraps himself in. Together, there is the possibility of balance.

In one audacious and enigmatic moment Cammell leads

us to believe that this union is consummated sexually. Coming down from his hallucinogenic trip, Chas falls asleep in the basement. We see Turner, in his green silk robe, seated on the floor of the room, watching him. The film cuts away to show Pherber and Lucy together in Turner's bedroom. We then see Turner lying on the bed next to Chas; the two figures lock in an embrace, and we see that the figure in the green silk robe is no longer Turner but Lucy.

Within this curious alchemy – this merging of performances – Cammell suggests, lies the redemption of both men. In dismantling Chas, Turner gifts him with self-awareness and reveals the essential truth of humanity that his 'performance' obscures – that the core of all things is the capacity to feel and to show love. Chas is transformed (a transformation which finds a curious echo in the very different 'conversion' in James Fox's life, from self-confessed 'privileged hippie' to evangelical Christian).

And what does Chas give Turner? The purification of death.

Performers, The

The seeds of the script that would eventually become *Performance* were sown in two preliminary outlines. The first, entitled *The Liars*, contains the germ of the story, but is barely recognisable from what *Performance* became. In brief, it tells the story of a Mafia-style gangster, Corelli, who has arrived in Paris to carry out a contract killing. The job completed, the police on his tail, he escapes to

London, where he rents a room in the Earls Court home of
a rock musician named Haskin, who has left his group, The
Spinal Kord, disillusioned with the commercial direction
their music is taking.

Also in Haskin's house is a runaway teenage girl named
Simon. Simon falls in love with Corelli, while Haskin
goes on a whistle-stop tour of the hot-spots of Swinging
London, in the course of which he meets an inter-
national groupie, Pherber, with whom he ends up in
bath and bed. And that's about as far the treatment
goes.

Some essentials of *Performance* are contained in the basic
plot – gangster meets rock star – and in some of the
characters, if not the characterisations (deciding to dispense
with the name of Haskin's group, The Spinal Kord, was
particularly prescient, given the advent of Spinal Tap a
few years later). But it is clearly a work-in-progress, half
conceived and unresolved – if striking for its evidence of
Cammell's eye for local detail. The milieux, clothing and
slang of hip London are all observed with fastidious accu-
racy: Earls Court, where Haskin lives in Trebovir Road,
is described as 'the megalopolitan camping ground. The
great public dossing-down, digging-in, holing-up facility
of South-West London'.

Simon, the teenage waif, is 'geared-out in a choice
assortment of scavenged finery from the Chelsea Antique
Market'. Haskin is described as not simply listening to
'rock' or 'pop' music, but to Otis Redding, James Brown
and John Lee Hooker. (Turner evidently shares his tastes:
sharp-eyed viewers will notice the Otis Redding album
lying on the floor of Turner's room when Rosebloom

makes his final check on the house after Chas has been apprehended.)

Sandy Lieberson: 'One of the things I loved about Donald was that he was so specific in terms of his observations and how to represent the film, through what kind of music and characters. There was something so precise about that that I knew he could direct the film. There was nothing vague or general. When we talked, everything was in specifics.'

It was this treatment that Cammell and Sandy Lieberson presented to Marlon Brando, in the hope that Brando could be persuaded to take the role of Corelli. Perhaps wisely, Brando passed.

Using *The Liars* as a skeleton, Cammell now began work on a new script, *The Performers*, which was written in London early in 1968. (Caroline Upcher, Cammell's PA at the time, remembers being summoned in the middle of the night to his rented flat in Eaton Mews, Belgravia, to transcribe his longhand notes. 'David Litvinoff would usually be there with him, talking all the time.') By now, Cammell had made up his mind that Jagger and Fox should play the leading roles, and the parts were clearly written with them in mind.

The Performers reads less like a film-treatment than an outline for a novel, interlacing dialogue with exposition, characterisation and textual digressions. It provides the most complete written guide to Cammell's thinking on the film that would become *Performance*. The key elements of the final film are very much in place: the character of Chas, and of his fellow thugs, Moody and 'Roseblum',

who is described as having '. . . an expressionless, well-
worn, Jewish face. A large, balding, cerebral head . . .'
(an uncannily accurate description of the actor Stanley
Meadows, who would later play the part). The character
of Pherber is directly carried over from *The Liars*. Simon,
the runaway, has become Lucy.

The story begins with Chas 'putting the frighteners' on
the owner of a Mayfair night-club, Lucifer's Pantry. Chas
drives a Ford Zodiac (later to be upgraded to a Jaguar). But
the camel-haired coat is already in place. And the sequence
where Chas and Moody pour acid over a Rolls-Royce
makes its first appearance.

Turner's house, in this version, is located not in Powis
Square, but in Melbury Terrace. Cammell establishes
Turner's place in the rock hierarchy with his tongue
firmly in his cheek. He was a big star, Mrs Gibbs tells
Chas, 'Bigger than Mick Jagger . . .'

Describing the first encounter between Chas and Turner,
Cammell makes clear that Turner quickly sees through
Chas's lie that he is a night-club entertainer. Chas's obvious
incompetence at juggling the balls that Turner throws him
dispels any doubts. But Cammell also draws attention to
some posters on the wall of the room – testifying to his
evidently encyclopaedic knowledge of, and enamourment
with, gangster lore – to signal Turner's recognition of the
true nature of Chas's 'performance'.

Turner is drawing the other curtain when he
becomes aware of the remaining beam of light. It
is falling on a poster on a wall. Like several of the

others, Pherber's 'early' work [she clearly dabbles in graphic arts], its images are those of archaic gangster violence; images of Chicago in the late 20s. Parts of dark men with Thompson guns, the bullet-riddled face of the Hawthorne Hotel, the classic South Italian faces under soft fedora hats – Joe Torrio, Drucci, Capone . . .

One of the faces is young, Irish, pale-haired; Dion O'Banion, the 'three-gun man'. (He had a slight smile as he regarded the photographer, with curiously wide-open eyes.)

At this moment, Turner knows what Chas is. His intuition is as lucid, as direct, as natural, as that very ordinary shaft of light.

Chas is limping towards the table on which £40 still lies. Turner says 'Wait a minute.' He tells Chas he can rent the room.

This reference to O'Banion is echoed further on in the script. The first outfit in which Turner and Pherber dress Chas to take his passport-photograph is a camel-hair overcoat and pale fedora, which, Cammell writes, is a 'verisimilarexactitudinous reproduction of true 1928 Chicago Loop District style'. Dressed in his new finerie, Chas 'looks fantastic. He's very solemn, poses in the mirror. In Turner's viewfinder, he is Dion O'Banion, the 3-gun man, the darlin' of Chicago, and 'Cock o'the North Side' (killer of 25 men) – with a moustache'.

The Performers deviates most radically from the finished film in its final third. Turner's exchanges with Chas are interrupted by the arrival of three visitors: Alexander, a fashionable art-tycoon (doubtless modelled on Robert Fraser); a woman named Lindy Sue-Dixon, who seems to be some sort of hippie jet-set adventuress, and a character called Mo-Joseph, described by Cammell as 'a dirty little Jew (in a quite literal sense), a stupendous musician, and Turner's best friend'. The three provide the opportunity for some period badinage about music, magic and star-signs.

Turner and Pherber leave the new arrivals and retreat to the bedroom where Chas is stoned and seduced. Afterwards, Turner and the now-disoriented Chas rejoin the new arrivals. Music is played. Turner dances, newly possessed by his exchanges with Chas. The mood is then broken by a peculiarly jarring, almost comical interlude, when the police arrive for a drugs bust. Fearing that the police will discover Chas's gun, Turner sacrifices his prime stash – 'vintage Atlas Mountains hashish . . . three ounces of the Acapulco Gold that he bought cheap off Donovan'. Chas, in his new hippie drag, goes unrecognised.

While Turner is taken off to the police station to make a statement, Lucy interrogates Chas on his true identity, and a relationship blossoms between them. She suggests he should hide out in the hippie haven of Marrakesh. 'There's definitely some fantastic outlaws there already – been there for years. And groovy people . . . Friends of ours – right, Pherber? They all went there last summer.'

Chas makes a telephone call to Tony, arranging for his passport-photos to be collected from a nearby café the next morning. He then has a final conversation with Turner, who has now returned from the police station. It is clear from the script that, at this stage, Cammell still had no precise idea of exactly how to summarise what has passed between them, how to resolve what has been gained and what lost.

'They say various things,' Cammell writes:

Which I cannot explain, and others which I cannot yet know. Before this point in this adventure is reached (by me, you, them) it will be apparent that these two have had, in the interminable thirteen hours that have passed since they met, a considerable effect on each other. Thus it is unlikely, for example, that Chas would ask, 'Why have you helped me, Turner?' . . . in words, that is. For in a certain way, he does ask. And in another way, equally clear, Turner will answer him.

Being Turner, if he said, 'Well, the fact is, I believe in Universal Love,' he would make it sound profoundly ironic; he would then indubitably say, '. . . so you see, I love you, Chas' (. . . 'It stands to reason, eh?').

They part and Chas goes downstairs to the basement, and Turner to his room, 'a little fatigued by the implacable intimations of Nemesis that he carries with him'. In the basement, Chas is joined by Lucy, and they make love. 'He keeps smiling and kissing her face with a sort of incredulous delight. He is gentle . . . he seems conscious of his extreme good fortune in being entrusted with this rare person.'

The following morning, Lucy delivers the passport-photos to the café. She is followed back to Powis Square by one of Flowers's gang. While Lucy takes a bath, Chas goes upstairs, where he is intercepted in the hall by 'Roseblum' and Moody. He is taken outside, where Harry Flowers waits in his Rolls-Royce. When Lucy comes upstairs to look for him, she encounters Turner, who tells her that Chas has gone . . . 'to America'. Cammell writes: 'He can't know, himself, whether it is true, or whether Chas has been taken back into some dark places, but I think he has an intimation of tragedy . . .'

Cammell adds: '(Does Chas leave a note . . . "Lucy – gone to Marrakesh, love, Chas").'

The script ends with Harry Flowers's Rolls-Royce driving slowly through Hyde Park. 'Morning sunshine, some kids on the way to school, a dog or two . . .'

Persia: See The Old Man of the Mountain

Pherber

Turner's girlfriend, played by Anita Pallenberg. Marianne Faithfull was originally in line for the role, but fell pregnant. Donald Cammell then turned to the American actress Tuesday Weld. Weld came to London to prepare for the role, but broke her shoulder and was forced to drop out. On reflection, Weld, an actress who made her name in teenage beach movies, seems an odd choice (a concession to Warner Bros, perhaps?). The fictional character of Pherber – utterly seductive, demonic, worldly-wise – seems so essentially drawn from the actual character of Anita Pallenberg that it is hard to imagine any other actress in the role.

In his first draft of *Performance*, entitled *The Liars*, Cammell describes Pherber as 'very direct, spontaneous, pithy, funny, rather arrogant, ironic more by accident than design, and at the same time elliptical and evasive when it comes to any questions about herself – sort of automatically secretive'.

From the moment of Chas's arrival on the Powis Square doorstep it is clear that Pherber holds the key to the relationship between the two men. It is she, after all, who admits Chas to the house in the first place. A moment's reflection is enough to tell us how implausible this is. A complete stranger appears on the doorstep, spinning a cock-and-bull story about being a friend of the musician tenant, Noel. One look at his battered face, his damaged hand, his hoodlum demeanour, would be enough to tell Pherber that he's not who he claims to be. Yet it is precisely this implausibility that hooks her interest.

'One fact [Chas] cannot guess,' Cammell writes in *The Performers*, is that 'Pherber, part cynic, part fantasist, was susceptible to his fortuitous choice of roles; the small mystery of a bleeding and beautiful Juggler dropped from a Fellini film into the basement . . . his pockets full of tinsel money, his eyes full of knives.'

We should not overlook the attraction of the 'tinsel money' – Pherber, it is clear, has a much more realistic understanding of the household's precarious finances than Turner does. But it is clear too that she has some intuition of the possibilities implicit in the relationship between the two men long before they are aware of it themselves.

In the kitchen of Powis Square, Turner reads Borges's

story 'El Sur' ('The South') aloud to Pherber and Lucy
(see **Jorge Luis Borges**). A parable of a man stepping
forward to meet his fate, it tells of Dahlmann, who
following a long illness is travelling to his home in the
South. He stops in a cantina, where he is challenged to
a fight by a young thug. 'At this moment,' Turner reads,
'something unforeseeable occurred. From a corner of the
room, the old ecstatic gaucho threw him a naked dagger
which landed at his feet. Dahlmann bent over to pick it
up. They would not allow such things to happen to me
at the sanitarium, he thought, and he felt two things – the
first . . .'

Pherber interrupts: '. . . Yessss, I know why.'

Turner: Why?
Pherber: Because you're afraid of him.
Turner: Yeah . . . Right baby . . . and he's afraid
too . . .
Pherber (taunts him): 'Of you?'

It is Pherber too who takes the lead in the 'dismantling' of
Chas's mind, picking the fly agaric mushroom and serving
it to him.

'How much did you give him?' Turner asks.

'Two thirds of the big one.'

'It's insane . . .'

But moderation and patience are not Pherber's style.
'I just wanted to speed things up . . . I want to get a
shift on.'

And it is Pherber who recognises that Chas's rigid sense
of his own masculinity is the key to his character – his

'performance' – and who purposefully seeks to subvert it through seduction.

In describing Pherber's encounter with Chas in *The Performers*, Cammell makes some illuminating points about her psychology, her need to manipulate and control, but also to be controlled – and what Chas can provide for her that Turner has long since lost.

> 'Who are you?' she asks. 'I dunno,' he says.
>
> She caresses his hair – her hair, on his head. 'This is your mask,' she says. She kisses him, touches him . . . with gentle salaciousness. It is apparent that it is still she who is controlling the movements of the game. 'Come here. I want to be entertained.'
>
> (She doesn't want to dominate him now. Her conquest of this figure of her fantasies, this real and actualised figure, can only be accomplished when he dominates her. Only then according to the rules can the violence which he incarnates be ritualised – re-incarnated – as love.)

Cammell goes on to suggest that ultimately it is Pherber that Chas 'has grown to understand most. She is certainly the tortuous path by which he has managed to reach a ledge on the fog-shrouded Chinese-landscape-mountain that is Turner's mind. (. . . The telescope, too, through which Turner has had a glimpse of the awesome hexagonal canyon that is Chas Devlin's soul.)'

Later in the same treatment, Cammell imagines a conversation between the two men in which Turner tells Chas: 'You should have made love to her, man.'

'Yeah ... but ... she's yours ... you know what I mean?' Chas replies.

'Well, she's yours as much as mine,' says Turner.

Does Pherber have any inkling of just how far the dangerous game that she and Turner are playing with Chas is likely to go? Probably not. While Turner greets the assassin's bullet with an expression of calm acceptance, Pherber recoils in horror. She is last seen, traumatised and blood-stained, cowering in the basement.

Powis Square

The choice of Powis Square, Notting Hill for the residence of Turner was a stroke of location genius. More louche than Chelsea (where Mick Jagger and Donald Cammell lived), more dangerous than Earls Court (where Brian Jones held court), Notting Hill's mixed population of working-class whites, blacks, Irish and a burgeoning hippie community lent the area precisely the whiff of seedy, down-at-heel bohemianism that Turner would choose to lose himself in.

An area of crumbling Victorian squares and terraces, Notting Hill had been immortalised a decade earlier by Colin MacInnes in his book *Absolute Beginners* as 'Napoli', a potential tinderbox of working-class white families and newly arrived immigrants from the Caribbean, which was to explode into the scene of Britain's first 'race riots' in 1958.

MacInnes described the area's

railway scenery, and crescents that were meant to twist elegantly but now look as if they're lurching

high, and huge houses too tall for their width cut
up into twenty flatlets, and front facades that it
never pays anyone to paint, and broken milk bottles
everywhere scattering the cracked asphalt roads like
snow, and cars parked in the streets looking as if
they're stolen or abandoned, and a strange number of
male urinals tucked away such as you find nowhere
else in London, and red curtains, somehow, in
all the windows, and diarrhoea-coloured street-
lighting – man, I tell you, you've only got to
be there for a minute to know there's something
radically wrong.

And what about the human population? The
answer is, this is the residential doss-house of our
city. In plain words, you'd not live in our Napoli
if you could live anywhere else.

Notting Hill was the stamping ground of the slum landlord
Peter Rachman, who built an empire on the ownership
of hundreds of properties in and around the area, and
who introduced a new word to the English vocabu-
lary, Rachmanism, which the *Concise Oxford Dictionary*
defines as 'the exploitation of slum tenants by unscrupulous
landlords'.

Rachman owed his fortune to the Rent Act of 1957,
which gave landlords licence to charge virtually what they
wished for a vacant room. This gave them a powerful
incentive to evict sitting tenants on fixed rents. Rachman's
team of rent-collectors and enforcers were given *carte
blanche* to drive out tenants either by intimidation or by
cutting off water and electricity supplies. The properties

were then subdivided into ever smaller units and re-let at inflated rents.

Rachman was quick to spot the potential for profit among the influx of new immigrants who began streaming into Britain from the Caribbean in the 1950s. Touts would wait at Waterloo station to steer new arrivals towards his properties – often the only accommodation available at a time when many landlords operated a colour bar. A typical example of Rachman's methods was his first major purchase in 1954. For £20,000 he acquired the lease on 1–16 Powis Terrace, a huge Victorian block, and installed a Nigerian landlord. Within months the block had been subdivided many times over to accommodate some 1,200 people. Rachman's willingness to let to black tenants was one reason for the growth of the black community in Notting Hill.

Among Rachman's most trusted lieutenants was Michael de Freitas, who was later to adopt the Muslim name of Jacob Abdul Malik (and later still the *nom de guerre* Michael X), and achieve notoriety as a self-styled Black Power leader (see *Lowndes Square*). De Freitas was in charge of Rachman's Powis Square properties, specialising in shift-letting and letting to prostitutes.

From property, Rachman expanded his activities into fraud and illegal gambling rooms. He was a familiar figure at gaming tables and in night-clubs, and his girlfriends included Mandy Rice-Davies and Christine Keeler, both of whom would subsequently gain notoriety through their involvement in the Profumo scandal, which broke a few months after Rachman's death in 1961.

By the end of the Sixties, when the film crew for
Performance moved into Powis Square, the combination of
cheap rents and the area's rough-and-ready, cosmopolitan
ambience had attracted a further wave of new arrivals –
hippies. The area around Portobello Road market and
Ladbroke Grove became London's closest equivalent to
San Francisco's Haight-Ashbury district.

Wholefood and 'head' shops and clothing emporia
crammed with the trove of journeys to the East lined
Portobello Road. The editorial offices of the underground
magazines *Oz* and *Frendz* were in the vicinity. And the
headquarters and studios of what was then England's
hippest record company, Island, were a two-minute walk
from Powis Square on Basing Street – convenient if
Turner was ever of a mind to resurrect his record-
ing career.

Notting Hill has undergone a massive wave of gen-
trification since the late Sixties. Many of the Victorian
properties converted by Rachman into flats have been
converted back to private houses, and are now occupied
by barristers and media figures. Art galleries and expensive
restaurants have colonised the side-streets off Portobello
Road. If *Performance* defined the mood of the area, albeit
glancingly, in 1968, it is now more accurately expressed in
the recent Hugh Grant and Julia Roberts vehicle, *Notting
Hill* – a romantic comedy about a bookseller who falls in
love with a movie star.

While Turner's home is supposedly number 81 Powis
Square, the exterior shots were actually of number 25.

If *Performance* were made today, he would more likely
be living across London, in Hoxton.

Première, The

Performance received its British première at the Odeon, Leicester Square in January 1971, as a benefit for the drugs advice charity, Release. To solicit support for the première, Caroline Coon, the head of Release, contacted Tony Elliot, the owner of *Time Out* magazine, which produced a special issue almost wholly devoted to the film, according it instant cult status.

Preview, The

The first public showing of *Performance* was a preview, organised by Warner Bros, at the Granada theatre in Santa Monica, California in July 1969. It was not a success.

Sandy Lieberson: 'It was a second-rate neighbourhood movie house, where they were playing *Midnight Cowboy*, which had been in release already – it was in its third or fourth run. In those days, the audience for a preview wasn't recruited as it is now. The film was simply put on after a scheduled performance, billed as a "major studio preview". So the audience had no idea what they'd be seeing; they weren't prepared. These were people who'd come to see *Midnight Cowboy*, six months after it had been released – neighbourhood people.

'The house was full. Very strangely, Ted Ashley, who was the chairman of Warners, was there; John Calley; all the publicity people. And they had invited the man who was the head of the ratings board of the Motion Picture Producers' Association, Dr Aaron Stern. He was a psychiatrist who was also a friend of Ted Ashley's.

'So it was a very tense atmosphere. First of all, the film

had been resurrected; this was its moment of truth. And the atmosphere wasn't right. It should have been at a first-run cinema, with a younger audience. Right from the start, with the scene of James Fox in bed with the mirror, making love to his girlfriend, you could feel there was an uneasiness in the audience. And then at the point where James Fox is being beaten by Joey Maddocks the audience just exploded. The beating was much more explicit in that edit, and longer; and people stood up and started shouting, "Get this off the screen." There was a huge uproar and they had to stop the film and offer people their money back. Some left. After twenty minutes they managed to re-start the film, but more people walked out.

'I was sitting between Joe Hyams, a good friend of mine from Warners, and another guy from publicity, and they grabbed hold of my arms saying, "Don't do anything; don't say anything."

'At the end of the movie, the Warners executives and Aaron Stern jumped up and left the cinema, and there was a big huddle outside. We were waiting around to see what would happen. We knew it was a disaster. It was pretty traumatic for all of us. The next day we had a meeting at Warner Bros, and they really didn't want to release the film. Stern had told them that this was too disturbing a movie. You have to remember the times. It was rather a docile period in cinema, certainly in mainstream, major studio cinema. Stern said this was terrible for Warner Bros to release this kind of movie, and there was no way in the world he would give it anything other than an X-rating. And Warners said that major studios had an agreement with the MPPA that major studios would not release

X-rated films. So they said there is a case for not releasing this film, ever. They insisted the film be re-edited.

'The way the film depicted violence and the way it used violence alongside sex, the way it questioned sexuality, male sexuality in particular – I think people found all of that very uncomfortable, very disturbing. We can look at it now and say, what was all the fuss about? But in 1969 people weren't as steeped in these sort of subjects through the movies as they are now. Now it all seems commonplace. But people said it was *dirty* – not pornographic, but *dirty*.'

R

Reviews, The

Performance was a film which divided critics, predictably arousing equal measures of praise and condemnation.

On the film's release in America, the *New York Times* ran two contrasting reviews in consecutive weeks.

Under the headline 'The Most Loathsome Film of All', lead reviewer John Simon lambasted the film.

You do not have to be a drug addict, pederast, sado-masochist or nitwit to enjoy *Performance*, but being one or more of these things would help. *Performance* is one of that new breed of movies that do not try to win you over by wit, seriousness, humour, plot, characterisation, logic, dialogue or any other such outmoded paraphernalia. Instead, the film is built up – if anything so slapped together can be said to be built – from shocks piled on shocks. Not surprises, which are a time-honoured device, not titillations, equally established, if somewhat less honourable, and not even shocks in the sense of bouts of honest-to-goodness indignation. Rather the film progresses by what I imagine a series of electro-shocks to be like, but a shock-treatment administered not by a therapist but by

a mis-programmed computer. The genre can only
be called the Loathsome Film.

A week later, another reviewer, Peter Schjeldahl, offered a
contrasting opinion under an equally provocative headline,
'The Most Beautiful Film of All?'

There are movies about violence and then there are
violent movies. *Performance*, that perfect, poisonous
cinematic flower, is a violent movie. It is not a movie
for everybody, but it is a very exciting movie and
for those who do not necessarily include sweetness
and light in their definitions of beauty, even a very
beautiful one as well. The principal pleasures of
Performance are those of its flesh. The inspired acting
of all hands, especially Jagger and Fox; Mr Roeg's
ravishing camera-work and an overall attention to
nuances of speech and gesture and decor, both
'significant' and purely ornamental, gives the movie
a texture as hypnotic in its density and intricacy as
a tantric mandala.

Two weeks after the film's release, Warner Bros attempted
to capitalise on this conflict of opinion by running an
advertisement in the *New York Times* which reprinted
both headlines.

Meanwhile, writing in the *Village Voice*, Andrew Sarris
described the film as 'In some ways . . . the most deliberately decadent movie I have ever seen. If movies had
odors, *Performance* would stink, but in an original way.'
Rolling Stone, which might have been expected to view

the film favourably, took a surprisingly hostile view. 'One of the attributes of evil is its ugliness, and on one level *Performance* is a very ugly film,' wrote the critic Michael Goodwin, adding that 'Hallucinatory though it may be I would not recommend seeing it while tripping.'

It was left to the *Hollywood Reporter* to offer the most unequivocal vote of praise, describing it as 'a brilliant, disturbing work of art'. The response was more measured in Britain. Writing in the *Guardian*, Derek Malcolm described *Performance* as 'richly original, resourceful and imaginative, a real live movie', and that rarest of things, a British film of 'outstanding quality', while Philip French in the *Observer* called it 'an urgent, mind-blowing revelation'. Writing in the *Daily Mail*, Cecil Wilson came up with perhaps the most improbable observation, noting that 'for most of the film – in which Jagger plays the part of a decadent pop star – he looks remarkably like Brigitte Bardot'.

The underground magazine *IT* described it as

> Probably the heaviest movie ever made: a kaleido-scope of transvestism, sado-masochism, death, bad fly-trips etc ... It's a totally illogical movie, a series of seemingly unrelated incidents and complex inter-relationships flashed across the screen at almost subliminal speed: Jagger-Fox; Jagger-chicks; Fox-chicks; chicks-chicks. Chilling and very effective with superb editing and camera-work.

Roeg, Nicolas (b. 1928)

Co-director and cinematographer of *Performance*.

After National Service in the army, Roeg worked as a stills-photographer, entering the film industry as a general factotum before graduating to camera-operator and, eventually, cinematographer on such films as *A Funny Thing Happened on the Way to the Forum* (1966), *Fahrenheit 451* (1966), *Far from the Madding Crowd* (1967) and *Petulia* (1968). Immediately prior to making *Performance*, Roeg had secured his first feature as a director, *Walkabout*. It was only because production on that was delayed that he was able to take on *Performance*.

Following *Performance*, Roeg went on to direct *Walkabout* (1971), *Don't Look Now* (1973), *The Man Who Fell to Earth* (1976) and *Bad Timing* (1980). These films, with their recurring themes of obsession and alienation, established Roeg as perhaps the most singular and adventurous of British film directors. In recent years, however, his work has met with a more equivocal critical response.

Roeg's attitude to *Performance* in the years since the film was made seems to be one of profound ambivalence. While Cammell was always happy to talk at length about the film, Roeg – increasingly weary perhaps of the debate about their respective contributions and importance to the film – has generally preferred to remain silent. Although it provided the starting-point for his directorial career, there is the sense that *Performance* has left some other, unspecified and more unhappy legacy. In a rare interview with Colin MacCabe of the British Film Institute, Roeg looked back at his collaboration with Cammell as a 'sort of secret exploration of our own brains' and a process of supporting 'each other in manipulation'. He went on to describe *Performance* as 'more than a movie', but a process in which 'without anybody knowing we changed our minds about life'.

Rolls-Royce

The classic British motor-car as status symbol. Tellingly, both Harley-Brown the barrister and Harry Flowers the gangster drive Rollers – a subtle statement on their attainments in their respective professions of the law and lawlessness. Harley-Brown's is black (old-school class); Flowers's is white (jumped-up, *nouveau riche* vulgarity). Harley-Brown's Rolls is first glimpsed passing along a country road, then parked outside a pub-restaurant where, we assume, Harley-Brown is enjoying a civilised business lunch. His chauffeur polishes the car as he waits. The chauffeur is next seen having his head shaved by Chas, Moody and Rosebloom while the car steams in a bath of sulphuric acid. Harry Flowers's Roller parks outside Turner's Powis Square house, ready to carry Chas to his fate. A luxury hearse.

Rosebloom

In the hierarchy of the Flowers firm, Rosebloom functions as regimental sergeant-major to Chas's first lieutenant, a stickler for procedure and correctness. ('Put your tie on . . .' he tells Moody, as they set out to rough up a mini-cab office.) While Moody is a thug, Rosebloom is an operator, a man who's seen it all before, and whose apparently quiet, unflappable demeanour conveys an altogether more subtle sense of menace. Notice the placatory gesture of bringing his finger to his lips to silence Harley-Brown while Chas menaces his client; notice the methodical way in which he goes about shaving the chauffeur's head – no need to make a fuss. There is a palpable note of regret in his voice as he apprehends Chas in the hallway of Turner's home. Dear, oh, dear. That it should come to this. But no room for sentiment. A job's a job, after all, and Rosie's a real old pro.

S

Shannon, Johnny (b. 1932)

The actor who plays Harry Flowers.

Before his appearance in *Performance*, Shannon had
worked for a wholesale newsagent, in Covent Garden
fruit market, as a trader on a fruit stall in Berwick
Street market, as a night-driver for newspapers and as
a runner for an illegal bookmaker. In the army he
had been in the boxing team with Henry Cooper (he
was among the helpers at the ringside when Cooper
fought his memorable bout with Cassius Clay); and in
his spare time Shannon trained boxers in the upstairs
gym at the Thomas A' Beckett, a famous boxers' pub
on the Old Kent Road. It was there that David Litvinoff
brought James Fox, in search of someone who could
tutor Fox in the dialect and manners of a London
hood.

Johnny Shannon: 'They wanted someone to take James Fox
around and advise him on the Cockney speech in his script.
I'd go through the script with him, I took him around the
Old Kent Road, the pubs and clubs, and introduced him
to some of the characters in South London. We taught
James how to hold a cigarette right – the chaps hold it
in a particular way; how to behave in a pub, call for a

drink. James was accepted into that crowd lovingly; they thought he was great.'

Fox was so impressed by his tutor that he suggested Shannon to Donald Cammell for the role of Harry Flowers.

'At first I took it as a joke,' Shannon told the *Guardian* in 1971. 'I thought it was a giggle really. I didn't know Mick Jagger was in it then. When I heard he was I thought straightaway, I shan't like him. But then when you meet him and get to know him he's a different fellow. He's a much nicer fellow. But I can't stand his music. I like singers like Dorothy Squires. Singers with feeling.'

Shannon's role in *Performance* led to a number of other acting parts, on television, usually playing the Cockney 'heavy', and in the films *The Villains* and *Flame*, starring the pop group Slade, in which he played the role of a sleazy agent.

Johnny Shannon: 'It did me a lot of favours, that movie. It got me work, which got me a couple of quid. In those days I was living in council flats. Now I've got a house in Kent.' Shannon later became a shareholder in a painting and decorating firm and continues to supplement his income with the occasional acting role.

Shoot, The

The filming of *Performance* started on 22 July 1968, in the Surrey countryside, with the film's opening sequence, showing Harley-Brown's Rolls-Royce driving along a country road to the Black Swan, Effingham Junction.

Filming then moved to the streets in and around the West End of London for the 'gangster' sequences. The exteriors of Harry Flowers's office were shot in Mount Street, Mayfair (the early-morning shot where we see the window of Flowers's office is actually of Robert Fraser's apartment). Flowers's 'bedroom' was the penthouse suite at the Royal Garden Hotel in Kensington; his 'office' was above a Chinese restaurant in Wardour Street; and 'the Hayloft Club', where Joey Maddocks is brought after his betting-shop has been destroyed, was actually a drinking club called the Latin Quarter, on Wardour Street. Maddocks's betting-shop was in the Fulham Road, a stone's throw from Chelsea football ground. Harley-Brown's chauffeur was kidnapped and shaved in Queen's Gate Mews, Belgravia. And the scenes at Paddington station, where Chas overhears the musician Noel talking about his basement flat, were shot not at Paddington but in the buffet of the car-rail terminal at Olympia.

Production then moved to Powis Square, Notting Hill and Lowndes Square, Knightsbridge for the exteriors and interiors of Turner's house. Turner's bedroom, bathroom and music room were all constructed in Lowndes Square. However, the basement scenes and 'Noel's room' were actually shot at a house in Hyde Park Gate, number 25. The set for Chas's apartment, where he is seen first seducing Dana and later murdering Joey Maddocks, was also located in Lowndes Square.

The early stages of filming, concentrating on the activities of Harry Flowers and Chas's flight, were relatively trouble-free. But, according to Sandy Lieberson, the atmosphere quickly changed from 'euphoric to manic depressive. It started off as great fun; we all had the highest expectations, but then the problems started with Warners.

'Getting a crew at all had been the hardest thing. It was the busiest summer, everyone seemed to be making movies; we ended up with an editor who had never done a feature before, I'd never produced a film before . . . We were filming with two cameras in a lot of places, and the film was just being churned out. Every day we'd end up with two and a half hours of rushes. Well, you just don't do that. Normally you take selected takes and you screen about twenty minutes of rushes for the studio executives. After just two weeks Warners went berserk because we were taking up so much time.'

David Cammell: 'The shoot was very tense, but not at all insane. The original idea was that we would take over Lowndes Square, install the cast and rehearse them for a week or two beforehand. But Mick was committed to something else and couldn't get away in time, so that didn't happen.

'It was a deliberate policy to shoot the entire film on location, which was very unusual for those days. We built sets inside the house [at Lowndes Square]. So it was boxes within boxes. And that created both physically and mentally a certain sort of pressure that added to the intensity of the performances and the atmosphere.'

*   *   *

The cast that assembled in Lowndes Square for the shoot-ing constituted a who's who of Donald Cammell's friends and lovers.

Cammell had slept with both Pallenberg and Breton. Jagger and Fox were close friends (a friendship that at one stage, according to Cammell, had blossomed into 'a little romance'). And Jagger was playing the lover of the girlfriend of one of his closest friends, Keith Richard (a combination which Cammell felt sure would 'hot things up'). On one level, the Lowndes Square shoot can be seen as Cammell's wilful manipulation of a series of existing and unresolved sexual tensions 'a psycho-sexual laboratory', as Marianne Faithfull would famously put it, with Cammell as the demonic scientist and the cast as his experimental animals.

Cammell himself always denied that he had such a 'research-oriented point of view'.

> I was more interested in seeing what happened. The curiosity wasn't entirely intellectual. It was a useful desire to make things happen – for internal combustion.
>
> I was infatuated by all these various literary and theatrical sources. Apart from the mythology of Borges and a contemporary recreation of the uni-verse in Borgesian terms, there was the Genet thing to do with homosexuality and art; there was the Artaud hobby-horse which I'd recently discovered – the Theatre of Cruelty. I really believed this was the way to create drama. I believed that a conviction

and determination to make things happen, and then conform to the rules that one imagines they conform to, is a good way to create drama.

I think the secret sex life of an actor is as much common and necessary terrain to use for creating drama as any other prop. An actor is a commodity; he hires himself. And whether he's Mick Jagger pretending to be an actor, or a young girl like Michèle who aspires to be a movie star, or a prematurely mature female adventuress such as Anita was, I wasn't aware of any rules and regulations about how you worked with people who were, for the purposes of the movie I was making, actors and actresses.

I didn't see I was infringing on any imaginary rights they might have had to have a private life. This idea that 'I'm an actor — my private life is private' is bullshit.

I remember preaching to Jimmy Fox, if you're a real actor you become the person you're acting, and then anything goes. You can do anything, because if Chas gets an idea or is provoked by a director to take a bath nude in the bird-bath in the middle of Lowndes Square then he will simply do it. Chas possesses the actor.

Any technique that works is OK; if you stir things up relentlessly you'll get results. And I went for it all the way. I thought the sparks were flying. They were all performers — and the idea of performance was alive and well and embodied by the title.

Christopher Gibbs: 'Donald is someone who believed in the fruitfulness of tension. There were a lot of couplings and uncouplings. People being wound up to do things. I think Donald was just trying to clear his head at the time. He basked in all these people who were rather younger than him. He loved all that. He loved the sexual chemistry, because that was one of his drives. I think he just saw that if you brought all these people together you would create something with this magical dimension, and he succeeded.'

One person who worked on the film, and prefers to remain anonymous, describes it as 'the most sexually charged film production ever. Everyone was fucking everyone. And Donald was a class-A voyeur.'

David Cammell: 'Donald had power, but not in a malicious way. But he was a bit of a control freak, definitely. That's why his films were so intense. He would take people and push them beyond their potential. He would get them so involved. That's what's interesting about his films; the actual making of them was a very intense experience. Everybody who got involved in it for good or ill would reel out of it wondering what had hit them.'

One of the first scenes filmed in Lowndes Square involved Jagger, Pallenberg and Breton in bed together. 'I never really fancied Mick,' Pallenberg remembers. 'We got along easy, but I didn't fancy him, but I found that whenever you make a movie and you have a partner, there's a little affair or something coming on . . .'

Keith Richard quickly learned of the 'little affair' and

would wait outside Lowndes Square in his Rolls-Royce, quietly fuming.

'Keith never came on the set,' Pallenberg remembers. 'But we used the same dealer. He'd report all the stuff that was going on. I'd go home every night and get a real slagging off.'

Sandy Lieberson: 'Keith Richard was very much against Mick being in the film. It was the first thing Mick had done outside the Rolling Stones, and Keith became very nervous about Mick and Anita getting involved. And, of course, that was exaggerated by Robert Fraser and that whole group saying Mick is going to end up in bed with Anita. It became a very difficult situation. It caused a real rift in the end.'

According to both Michèle Breton and Anita Pallenberg, hashish was being consumed in copious quantities on the set.

'It was all very psychedelic,' says Pallenberg. 'I remember we had Booker T music playing all the time, and there was a lot of waiting, and a lot of prima donna stuff from Donald, coming in and slamming doors. The actors were like little lambs. Sometimes tempers were flying, particularly Donald. Nic would come in and talk us through a scene first, and then Donald would come in and tell us something completely different. The directors were the prima donnas. I remember once after a scene asking, "Did I say my line?" and everybody being really furious because I didn't know whether I'd done my line or not. But it was . . . y'know, loads of joints and stuff. It was like that.'

Breton, in particular, seemed unnerved – a stoned, anxious presence. 'There was a feeling that people were set up, the friction of the characters against one another,' Pallenberg remembers. 'Michèle Breton was so paranoiac about me and Mick, for example. She thought we were scheming against her. I remember sometimes even before a scene she had to have a doctor give her an injection to calm her down. It was paranoia.'

For her part, Pallenberg was jealous of the attention that Breton was being given by the two directors. Breton was already involved with Cammell, but Pallenberg suspected that Nic Roeg had also taken a liking to her.

Donald Cammell: 'Anita was very hard on Michèle, because Michèle was younger. Maybe there was some jealousy there, and Anita could be very mischievous, very smart – very witchlike, as she used to think.'

For Cammell, the personal relationship between Fox and Jagger was a crucial element in developing the fictional exchanges between Turner and Chas.

I was talking about losing all self-consciousness, all consciousness and, if necessary, control in order to embody people who were at the very edge of their existence; people who were playing a game of life and death for their psychic survival.

Jagger was supposed to be a guy on the edge of lunacy, and trying to grab at poetic ideas of being possessed by someone else's demonic energy; a young male animal that comes into his febrile, evanescent world where he was wasting away for lack of stimulus. These dangerous games had to be performed with a great deal of authenticity. I remember Mick saying, 'You're completely bonkers – what the fuck are you talking about, Donald?' But at the same time he did do it, and he's never done it since except as a rock star. It's very difficult for Mick to lose his self-consciousness.

'[Donald and I] had terrible rows because I didn't think he knew what he was doing,' Mick Jagger told *Time Out* in an interview in 1970.

He'll probably say that I didn't really either. Roeg was the professional doing his thing. He was always reliable and he had his little lighting cameraman job to do as well . . . Donald wrote the story and he was the driving force as far as the actors were concerned. Between the two they were working out the delineation of their authority.

You had to know what you were doing before you got on camera. It wasn't just a question of improvising for hours and hours. We had to work it out otherwise you just got in a mess. We'd suddenly stop shooting one day because I'd say I wasn't going to say those lines. There were all kinds of situations like that and the regular technicians would go, 'Blimey, I've never seen anything like it!' and all that. Donald's whole thing is casting people for what they are and how they fit into the part, to make them work and create the part, rather to work on the things that were already in their minds.

Thanks to his fitness regime in the Thomas A' Beckett, James Fox, according to Donald Cammell, 'looked like the most handsome man on earth', a fact which, Cammell detected, caused some feelings of jealousy in Jagger.

Mick was hard on Jimmy because of the romance; he was teasing him about that, playing with him to a certain extent. Off-set as well he was teasing him in this trivial, stupid way: wise-cracks, working-class jokes. He liked to get at Jimmy because he'd always get a rise out of him. He'd tease Jimmy about pretending to be tough. And Jimmy took that badly. The whole thing became very explosive. Jimmy was working some things out in his own mind. That went on for the first five weeks of shooting, and after that Jimmy got on top of it and sort of put Mick in his place. There were times when they almost came to blows.

There was a tremendous tension between them. They were both scaring themselves, and scared of looking absurd. I remember getting this big mirror and making Jimmy really study himself for half an hour. He was scared of putting on the wig – 'I'll look funny,' he'd say. But by really looking at himself he just became hypnotised by the strangeness and beauty of his own image. He got the balls where he could dominate the atmosphere on the set. And dominate Mick.

David Cammell: 'Mick started really teasing James, perhaps because he was a bit jealous of James being a professional.

In fact, at one point James walked off the set and absolutely refused to perform with Mick.'

For Fox, the Lowndes Square shoot was to prove particularly traumatic. Apart from Pallenberg, who had some limited acting experience, Fox was the only one among the principals who could be described as a professional actor (a deliberate policy by Cammell). Determined to maintain standards of professionalism, he would diligently learn his lines, only to turn up next day to discover that Cammell, responding to the creative imperatives of the moment, had completely rewritten the script.

Fox was also grappling with a personal tragedy. His father, Robin – who was also his agent – was dying of cancer while the film was being made, and he was also extremely anxious about his son's well-being. 'Robin was deeply disturbed that the script kept changing all the time, and he didn't know what he'd let his son in for,' says David Cammell. 'Robin died soon afterwards, and that scarred James terribly.'

In the face of mounting strain, Fox took refuge in pro-fessionalism, spending hours in his dressing-room, studying the script, struggling to find some balance between himself – the confused 'privileged hippie' – and his role as the repressed, fascistic Chas.

In her role as Pherber, however, Anita Pallenberg says that she 'was just playing myself'.

Most of the stuff I speak, when I try to freak out James Fox on the bed, that was all my own stuff. I had a free rein in my dialogue . . . like when I'm bandaging James's body.

I remember when James was doing the mushroom scene, I asked him, 'Have you tried any acid?' He kept on saying, 'No, no, I know how to do it.' And I kept on saying, well Method acting – you have to really know, you've got to experience it. I was always threatening to put acid in his coffee – keep him on his toes, y'know?

James had a little room off to one side, with a table, and I remember him in there, just buried in the script. I wasn't that kind of actress. For me it was just have a good time. I think I irritated him a lot because of that. My relationship with him wasn't good. And Jagger was very insecure. It was his first film, so he started off imitating James. Then he saw what I was doing and started to loosen up and get stoned. More happy-go-lucky.

In her autobiography, Marianne Faithfull would provide a vivid description of what she regards as one of the key 'subplots' to the making of *Performance*. 'What would happen if you took a repressed upper-class Englishman and loaded him up with a bunch of psychotropic drugs, played mind games with him, buggered him and then put him in a film that recapitulates all this (but with genuine gangsters)? James Fox was, to say the least, slightly out of his element.'

Fox himself would be amused by the analysis. 'I don't recognise all that Marianne's saying, but it's an interesting spin.'

It was true, he said, that Jagger and Pallenberg 'would play with me and try and mess me up. But what's very interesting about that is there's a kind of discipline and control about art. Whereas in life I certainly had my mind screwed up in lots of different ways prior to *Performance*, when it came to the film, because I was anchored in the reality of Chas, I felt much more in control.'

One long-standing point of discussion about the shoot concerns the division of labour between Donald Cammell and Nic Roeg. Broadly speaking, Cammell's role was in developing the script and 'priming' the actors before shooting took place. Roeg, the technician, was responsible for 'the look' of the film, and would take charge of the action once the cameras had started rolling.

Photographs taken on set show the difference between the two men: Cammell, the creative maverick, tousle-haired, and dressed in jeans and a pullover; Roeg, the professional, invariably dressed in a blazer, shirt and tie.

The atmosphere between the two men was not always cordial. 'It was a highly charged atmosphere,' remembered Mike Molloy, the camera-operator. 'There were quite long rehearsals, and the crew would often be banished while various artistic differences were sorted out.'

According to one crew member, at one stage Roeg took to wearing a raincoat to the shoot each day and at strategic moments would make a show of buttoning it up, as if making ready to leave, to make Cammell nervous.

'Donald and Nic were two sides of the same coin, both real operators,' remembered one participant. 'Donald loved mixing it; he loved to provoke, and he was very naughty. He was the puppet-master, but in a very charming way. Nic had the capacity to gain the respect of people – technicians and cameramen and so on, because he knew what he was talking about. He was straight in that respect.'

So, whose film is *Performance*? The conception, the script, the characterisations, the peculiar and explosive chemistry of ideas and moods that drive the film – all of these are clearly Donald Cammell's. But it required the professional expertise and 'the eye' of Nic Roeg to bring all those elements to fruition.

Ironically, perhaps, it was to be Roeg who benefited most from the film. While Cammell struggled to edit the film under pressure from Warner (see **The Edit**), Roeg went off to Australia to complete his first feature, *Walkabout*. And as Roeg's career blossomed, and Cammell's faltered, so it came to be popularly believed that Roeg was the principal architect of *Performance*.

This became a cause of some rancour for Cammell. 'Donald never talked about it until quite late in his life,' says David Cammell, 'but it was upsetting for him. *Performance* absolutely propelled Nic's career. Donald must have resented it, but he never criticised Nic in public for that.'

On reflection, it is extraordinary quite how much latitude the directors and producers were allowed by Warner. They were trusted to shoot the film entirely on location with virtually no studio supervision. And for a long time, it seems, Warner was oblivious to what was actually occuring on the Lowndes Square set, and how controversial the film would actually be.

Sandy Lieberson: 'Ken Hyman [Warner's head of production in London] didn't see the rushes of the film for some time. Ray Anzarat [Hyman's production supervisor] and several other people, including people who worked on the distribution side, would come in to see the rushes after lunch. And most of them would promptly fall asleep.

'We had an inexperienced editor working on the film. The normal process when you're showing rushes is to show selected takes, not every bit of film that's shot during the day. The editor didn't do that. Everything was shown in its raw form. So our rushes sometimes ran for two hours or more. Eventually, at some point – I think it was the bath scene – somebody from Warners said, hey wait a minute, this is going too far. And that's when Ken Hyman got involved and said, this is not going to continue.'

In a subsequent interview with Derek Malcolm in the *Guardian*, Donald Cammell recalled that Hyman was 'horrified' by what he saw when he finally visited the set. 'He looked at Mick Jagger and shouted to a henchman, "Hey, Dave, this guy is bi." He said it was the dirtiest movie he'd ever seen and wanted to stop shooting there and then.' Shooting was abandoned for a weekend, but eventually Cammell, Roeg and Lieberson were able to persuade Hyman to let them complete the film.

Sandy Lieberson: 'Nic was very helpful in that respect. He was the one figure in the group who at least was professional, so to speak, who had some film experience, and could calm Ken Hyman down. And we were allowed to keep going. In the end, we went eight or nine days over schedule. The film cost one and a half million dollars, and we ended up about $150,000 over budget, which was really nothing. Mick Jagger got well paid by his standards. We all did. As producer and a former agent I made sure we were all well-paid. There was very little money left to actually make the movie.'

Production on *Performance* was finally completed in twelve weeks. Donald Cammell would describe the process, without the slightest irony, as 'a fabulous shoot'.

Sidney, Ann (b. 1944)

British actress who played the role of Chas's girlfriend, Dana. Sidney was a hairdresser from Poole when she won the Miss World contest in 1964. *Performance* was to be her biggest film role. She went on to act in repertory on the stage in Britain, and to perform as a cabaret entertainer in Las Vegas.

> *Performance* was my first film role. All I knew about the film from the script was that I had a scene with James Fox. The scenes were shot in a flash. I was very frightened – and he was too – of doing the love scene. Nudity was frowned on in those days and we both felt very uncomfortable about it, but it was fine. Nic Roeg shot the scenes and he was awfully nice.
>
> From my point of view, it was a little frightening to play that role. I was playing a singer who had met someone she was attracted to and he treats her badly. The typical, classic situation of a man being out for one thing alone and saying goodbye in the morning.

But it made sense in establishing the character of Chas, as far as his main desires, his wants, where he was going, the fact that he had no respect for women. It made a statement straight away.

I think those scenes were a little hotter than some of the scenes shown today because that's how Donald and Nic wanted the film to be; they wanted to make it different, very cult-orientated, rather shocking. That was the point they wanted to get across, and it was the point we got across.

I've only ever seen the film once. The decadent side of it didn't appeal to me personally at all, but I learnt something from it. I learnt it wasn't my life-style.

Simpson, Don (1945–96)

Legendary Hollywood producer of such 'high-concept' films as *Flashdance, Top Gun* and *Beverly Hills Cop*, who died in 1996 at the age of fifty-two from a heart attack. Simpson's first job in Hollywood was working in the marketing department of Warner Bros, where he organised a press screening for *Performance*, renting an exhibition space and buying two pounds of marijuana and twenty cases of cheap red wine. 'The movie became the talk of the town,' he said later. 'Why not? Everybody was loaded.'

Soundtrack, The

Co-ordinated by Jack Nitszche. Music conducted by Randy Newman. Performed by: Randy Newman, Ry Cooder, Bobby West, Russell Titelman, Milt Holland,

Amiya Dasgupta, Lowell George, Gene Parsons and the Merry Clayton Singers.

Donald Cammell originally wanted the Rolling Stones to provide the soundtrack for *Performance*. Keith Richard's resistance to Jagger taking part in the film, and his growing suspicions about what was happening on set, put paid to that idea. But Richard did provide an alternative. The Hollywood composer and arranger Jack Nitzsche had produced a soundtrack for the film version of Terry Southern's novel *Candy*. It was not used, but Nitzsche played the soundtrack to Richard, who was sufficiently impressed to suggest that he might provide a similar service for *Performance*.

In lieu of the Rolling Stones, Nitszche recruited a band of LA session musicians, including Ry Cooder, Lowell George and Randy Newman. The strength of the subsequent soundtrack lies in its dazzling eclecticism: the hard rock of Randy Newman's 'Long Dead Train'; the proto-rap of 'Wake Up Niggers', by the Harlem group the Last Poets; the haunting mouth-bow playing and singing of Buffy Sainte-Marie – as exotic as the Christopher Gibbs furnishings in Turner's house; the exquisite and evocative bottleneck-guitar of Ry Cooder. (Jagger was so impressed with Cooder that, a year later, he was among the candidates for the vacancy in the Stones created by the death of Brian Jones. Cooder turned the offer down.)

The most arresting element of the soundtrack, however, came with the acquisition by Nitzsche of a prototype Moog synthesiser, which he played himself with one finger. The pulsating sound of the Moog is first heard in the film's opening moments, as the action rapidly intercuts between images of Harley-Brown's Rolls-Royce and Chas and Dana engaging in frantic sex – a cipher for dislocation – and is heard periodically thereafter as an exclamation mark heightening the audience's sense of disorientation as the drama unfolds. The voice heard in the film's closing moments as Turner/Chas walks towards Harry Flowers's Rolls-Royce belongs to Merry Clayton, a ubiquitous Los Angeles session singer of the day, who also provided the spine-tingling vocal on the Stones' song 'Gimme Shelter'. It's just a kiss away . . .

T

Telegram, The

When Ted Ashley, the chairman of Warner Bros in Los Angeles, first saw *Performance* he was appalled. Ashley immediately ordered that the film should be radically edited if there was any chance of it being released. Donald Cammell tried to mobilise support for the film, petitioning Stanley Kubrick, garnering letters of support from Kenneth Anger and David Maysles, and enlisting Mick Jagger's help to dispatch a telegram of protest to Ashley.

Re *Performance*:
This film is about the perverted love affair between Homo Sapiens and Lady Violence. It is necessarily horrifying, paradoxical and absurd. To make such a film means accepting that the subject is loaded with every taboo in the book.

You seem to want to emasculate (1) the most savage and (2) the most affectionate scenes in our movie. If *Performance* does not upset audiences it is nothing. If this fact upsets you, the alternative is to sell it fast and no more bullshit. Your misguided censorship will ultimately diminish said audiences in quality and quantity.

Cordially, Mick Jagger, Donald Cammell.

Ashley never replied.

Thomas A' Beckett

Famous boxers' pub in the Old Kent Road, South London. It was here, in the gymnasium upstairs, that James Fox was whipped into shape by Johnny Shannon for his role as Chas.

The pub was also used as a location for the telephone conversation between Chas and his friend Tony when Chas goes on the run from Harry Flowers.

The Thomas A' Beckett closed its doors as a pub and gymnasium for the last time in 1996 and was most recently in use as a Malaysian restaurant and wine-bar.

Turner

In the scabrous bathroom of his basement flat in Turner's house, Chas is washing his hair and talking to the precocious Laraine about Turner's rock career.

'He wasn't that big,' says Chas. 'I remember him quite well.'

'He was an' all,' replies Laraine. 'He was world famous, wasn't he? When I was a nipper. He was a chart-buster . . . I fancied him myself – old rubber lips. He had three number ones and two number twos and a number four.'

Chas interrupts. 'Didn't last though, did it? His success . . .'

It seldom does.

What has led to Turner withdrawing from the rock arena and secluding himself in his crumbling mansion? Not the fickle appetites of his public, it seems, but his own inertia and ennui. Turner is terminally jaded. His muse and his energy have deserted him; he has exhausted the possibilities of his art, grown tired of its rewards and bored with its diversions. He can vamp on a variation of a Robert Johnson blues, but where's the gift that made him a star?

'Why don't you play a tune?' says Chas. But Turner can't be bothered. 'I don't like music,' he replies in the voice of a bored child.

The observation of Noel's mother that 'He can't face reality' is true, but not in the sense she means. Turner's retreat is not from the 'reality' of the 'straight' world and its values; it is a retreat from the truth of his failure as an artist.

Pherber – canny, witchy, wise Pherber – puts her finger on it in one of the film's defining lines: 'He's lost his demon.'

It's time for a change. And Chas is the catalyst. As Pherber, again, puts it: 'He wants to know why your show is a bigger turn-on than his ever was.'

By 1968, when Cammell wrote *Performance*, the potentially debilitating consequences of rock fame were evident for all to see. The Beatles had stopped performing, tired of the exertions of the road; Brian Wilson was on the edge of psychedelic madness, and Phil Spector already secluded behind the walls of his Bel Air mansion, lost in the mists of deranged hubris. Within a couple of years, the roll-call of the dead would begin to mount: Joplin, Hendrix, Morrison – and Brian Jones.

The easy assumption is that Turner is simply an extension of Mick Jagger, but Jones is a more useful starting-point in examining the provenance of the character.

Jones was the founding-member of the Rolling Stones and the group's most gifted musician. But by the time of

Performance he was a busted flush. Demoralised by drugs, and a paralysing sense of his increasingly precarious place within the Stones hierarchy – painfully symbolised by his loss of Pallenberg to Keith Richard – Jones had become a shambling, pathetic figure, too stoned even to play on the group's recordings.

It was Cammell's fascination with Jones that had first brought him into the orbit of the Rolling Stones. He knew Jones well, and was able to witness his deterioration at first hand. And while Turner hardly reflects Jones's state of hapless dereliction, his character is certainly steeped more in the guitarist's fatigue than it is in Mick Jagger's steely determination and resolve.

In his book *Up and Down with the Rolling Stones*, 'Spanish Tony' Sanchez, the Stones' sometime dealer (and not an altogether reliable witness), describes a conversation where Marianne Faithfull coaches Jagger for the role:

'Whatever you do, don't try to play yourself. You're much too together, too straight, too strong. You've got to imagine you're Brian: poor, freaked-out, deluded, androgynous, druggie Brian. But you also need just a bit of Keith in it: his tough, self-destructive, beautiful lawlessness. You must become a mixture of the way Brian and Keith will be when the Stones are over and they are alone in their fabulous houses with all the money in the world and nothing to spend it on.'

Faithful herself offers a more complete account in her autobiography. Never having acted before, Jagger, she suggests, 'didn't have the faintest idea' how to approach the role. He knew, of course, how to act Mick in 'real'

life, but his character in the film was another thing
entirely.

'My reading of Turner was a symbolic figure,' Faithfull
writes.

> Vaguely tragic, a little pathetic, but still with an
> edge. He was the archetypal sixties rock apocalypse
> character, a pre-Raphaelite Hamlet. We worked it
> out very carefully and put it together, element by
> element.
>
> I suggested Mick start forming his character based
> on Brian, but to dye his hair. His hair should be a
> very strong, definite colour. To do Turner as a blond
> would have been too much. In the end he dyed it
> black, very black, a Chinese black, like Elvis's hair.
> Brilliant. Straight away it gave him a strong graphic
> outline. His tights and costumes gave him a tinge of
> menace, a slight hint of Richard III.
>
> The idea of using Brian as the basis for Turner was
> a good start, but as soon as he began rehearsing the
> script it was obvious that this was too simplistic . . .
> So we thought what about Brian and Keith? Brian
> with his self-torment and paranoia and Keith with
> strength and cool.

'Behind this characterisation of Turner', Faithfull continues:

> Was the feeling that Mick's personality was not dark
> enough or damaged enough to support a mythic
> character such as Turner. Turner was a sort of

jaded Prince of Denmark, but Mick was no Prince
Hamlet. There's nothing truly mythic or tragic
about Mick, he's too normal for any truly bizarre
fate to befall him. Brian and Keith seemed, if not
actually tragic figures, at least fated personalities,
human beings with fatal flaws caught in the tow
of deep undercurrents.

Faithfull admits that in encouraging Jagger to forge a
hybrid of Jones and Richard in his characterisation of
Turner, she did not anticipate the effect this would have on
Anita Pallenberg, 'that Mick, by playing Brian and Keith,
would be playing two people who were extremely attractive to Anita, and who were in turn obsessed with her'.

Anita Pallenberg: 'Mick dyed his hair black, like Keith's, but
there wasn't that much of Keith's character. And the way
he talked, all lah-de-dah, up in the air, was like Brian. It
was the way Mick would have liked to see himself. But the
character was degenerate and decadent . . . it was acting. In
those days Mick wasn't so decadent, but maybe he picked
up something from that. After *Performance* he was like the
little lord all of a sudden. The lad turned into a lord. I
think that was a conscious change. It was what he was
after – social climber kind of thing. Mick's whole thing
was calculating.'

So Turner is an amalgam. Jagger himself has said that
he based his performance partly on Brian Jones, but partly
too on Donald Cammell, 'though I don't think he knew'.
Cammell claimed that Turner's lisp came from Cammell's
imitations of Robert Fraser. 'I always imagined Turner as

a working-class guy who aspired to this aristocracy. And there was a lot of aristocracy in his presence, I think.'

Jagger elaborated on the character in an interview with *Time Out* magazine in 1970, where he described Turner as

> a projection of Donald's fantasy or idea of what I imagine how I am. The thing is that it's very easy for people to believe that's what I'm like. It was easy to do in a way because it's just another facet of me if I felt inclined to go that way. But now when I look at it there's so many things I could have done to make it stranger or to make it more real, to my mind, of how Turner would be and how he would live. I think it was a bit too much like me in a few ways. But he's not quite hopeless enough.
>
> . . . I found his intellectual posturing very ridiculous – that's what sort of fucked him up. Too much intellectual posturing in the bath when you're with two women is not a good thing – that's not to be taken too seriously! It made me skin go all funny! . . .

But whatever elements of friends and acquaintances – or himself – were woven into Jagger's portrayal, Turner is essentially a compendium of, and a vehicle for, Donald Cammell's enthusiasms, hobby-horses and obsessions; his fascination with violence and the dynamics of performance, with Borges, with magic, with sex.

'I realized that *Performance* was a movie that would throw a lot of things in the face of the audience,' Cammell told the BBC some thirty years after the film was made. 'I wasn't trying to make a statement of any kind. I was trying to show the ingredients of an unstructured world that was Turner's and his groping with a perception of reality. His experiments with sex, and his ideas about love and so on were part of the culture of the time, but they'd never been presented so graphically, or so elegantly, before. And I'm very proud of that.'

V

Valentine, Anthony

British actor, familiar from scores of film, television and theatre productions. Valentine plays the part of Joey Maddocks.

Making *Performance* was a very vivid experience. I don't know whether anybody else has mentioned this, but it was quite a druggy scene. And if you didn't do it as part of your professional life there was a kind of divide. You were on one side or the other. I was on the other side. I remember one of the technicians coming into Lowndes Square one morning and saying, 'Where's the fucking catering then?' And somebody else saying, well they're not here yet. 'No fucking catering? It's the fucking limit. You want to get a fucking joint, they're coming out of your ear-holes. You want a cup of tea you've got no fuckin' chance!'

Ostensibly I was signed for something like three weeks over five. The betting-shop and night-club sequences were shot early on, so my involvement in the house in Lowndes Square ostensibly should have been minimal, because it only involved a certain number of scenes which were the beating up of

Chas. But that was where I spent the other six weeks
or whatever, waiting to finish those scenes. It made
it frustrating and rather boring for me. I was called
every single day, first up, and was still there at nine
in the evening, in full costume and make-up, sitting
around reading a book, drinking tea and eating buns,
while they were upstairs in another room deciding
how to do a particular scene that might not even be
in the script. It was that fluid.

I've never been involved in a movie like that
before.

Don and I always had an extremely uncomfortable
relationship, because I was a bit too, I think, plebeian
for Don. A bit too prosaic. For instance, in the
sequence where Joey and his cohorts beat up Chas
– and I can't believe this even while I'm telling you
– Don wanted me stripped to the waist and oiled
up. For me, playing the part was a question of 'show
me the marks, show me the lights and I'll act it for
you' – but, please, don't give me all this crap about
being oiled. I said to Don, how did I suddenly get
stripped to the waist and oiled up? Don's language
was always that Sixties thing of 'Hey, come on, man'
. . . the mid-Atlantic accent. 'I'm talking about a
visual thing.' I said, I've just got to tell you, Don,
that when they see me in the ABC Fulham on
a Saturday night, pulling James Fox's underpants,
whipping him with a dog lead, and I'm stripped to
the waist with my body oiled, you're not going hear
the next fifteen minutes of the movie. And with the
rain of stuff that's being thrown at the screen, you're

not going to see it either. And of course he went ape-shit about that as he did about other things. But it wasn't Joey Maddocks; it wasn't honest.

Don and I really didn't get along. I couldn't subscribe to all that King's Road poncing about in three-quarter-length white coats and black fedoras. It made me very uncomfortable.

The first time I went to see him he said, 'I'm having a lot of trouble with this part, man. I must have tested every boxer in London and none of them can act.' I said, isn't that extraordinary! And probably you've got all these actors in that can't box. Isn't life peculiar . . . Finally, on about the third interview, he said, with as much charm as he could muster, 'Tony, I think you're going to have to do this because I can't find a boxer who can act, so let's just hope you can box.' The guy was so far up my nose I could hardly breathe even before we started the movie.

The fight sequence was finally shot on the set in Lowndes Square. They'd set aside three days for it. Donald said, 'I just want this to happen.' No planning, no forethought. Now James and I got along extremely well together and we both knew that you cannot Mickey Mouse fights, because somebody will get hurt. You've got to choreograph them like a ballet. I asked Don who was staging this, and he looked at me and gave me this 'are we all going to dance around like faggots?' shtick. My sidekicks were these two guys from the Thomas A' Beckett – a couple of very strong, very fit lads, both boxers – both of them obviously thinking, what a wonderful game; we're going to give James Fox a smacking. So I said, what's it going to do to you, Don, if James is out of the picture for three days with a broken nose? He said, 'For fuck's sake. Will you just go in and do it.' And that turned into the ugliest row of the entire movie.

I said to James that I was going to do the utmost to look after myself and he said, 'Don't worry about me, Tony.' He and I sorted it out that as we walked through the door I would grab him and these other two guys would rush him. And on the first take, in the mêlée, one of these guys got a broken nose and the other one got three cracked ribs, and that was the end of the take. After three months working out at the Thomas A' Beckett James was as hard as the Rock of Gibraltar, and there was no way he was going to stand still for a smacking simply because some director with a fantasy didn't want to rehearse it. He wanted 'real'. Well, that's what he got. He also had to get another couple of lads from the gym before he could have another crack at it.

I think a lot of people on the movie got very disturbed by the violence, because there was a very heavy, very intense atmosphere of only barely suppressed violence, which occasionally would just break the surface.

There is a story which I believe to be true about the scene where they pick up the chauffeur and shave his head. They'd got John Sterland, who played the chauffeur, to agree to have his head shaved, but they didn't tell him how it was going to happen. Apparently, in shaving his head not only did John get cut, but they kept him tied up on the chair while they had a tea-break and they didn't give him any tea. And I heard that somebody actually kicked the chair over while he was in it. The whole point being – and it's back to Donald Cammell's idea – 'don't let's organise this; let's make it real'. So it ain't going to hurt the guy if he doesn't get a cup of tea, and if he gets upset it'll look good on camera. And people went along with that.

I think by the end of that movie there were a lot of people who couldn't actually manage to suspend their disbelief any more. People who were saying, 'What the fuck are we doing here?' Because what I think was actually happening in the second half of the movie was the acting out of one man's fantasies. So if Cammell wanted something that was violent and awful, that was what you did. If he wanted something that was extremely and intensely sexual, that was what happened. If he wanted something that was an ode to the drug culture, that was what happened. If the movie had a sub-text it was that there was no-one to say 'no'. And I think, in a way, one began to feel like a slightly underpaid whore. In other words, this somehow isn't about acting any more. It's about taking part in a rather black fantasy that this man is putting together, and for doing that I'm not being paid enough.

I don't think 'like' is a word I could use about *Performance*. I remember at the première it was met by a stunned silence. People sort of didn't know what to make of it. It was a brand leader. Donald put together a unique movie which changed the direction of at least some movie making. The first half of the movie, which is actually a straightforward thriller, is terrific, I think. In the second half, I wasn't sure I quite understood what was going on.

Vice. And Versa

The slogan used on the posters advertising *Performance* on its British release in 1971. Playing on the film's theme of sexual ambiguity, the posters showed four images of Jagger's and Fox's characters: Turner in full make-up, and with slicked-back hair, suit and tie in the 'Memo From Turner' sequence; and, below that, Chas as clean-cut gangster and wearing his long-haired wig. The copy below reads: 'See them all in a film about fantasy. And reality. Vice. And Versa.'

Vitamin B12

Talking with Turner, Pherber hikes up her dressing-gown and sticks a hypodermic syringe in her buttock – an ominous portent of what was to come. The post-production script has Turner saying, 'In my opinion, darling, you're much too healthy'; to which Pherber replies, 'Too much vitamin B12 has never hurt anybody.' Turner's line was subsequently changed to the more ambiguous 'You shoot too much of that stuff.'

Anita Pallenberg: 'That shot was done after everything else. At the time I had a dealer, Spanish Tony, who would bring me drugs on the set. I was getting stoned most every day, because of the boredom and tedium. Nic Roeg would take about seven hours to set up a shot, so I'd get stoned basically. Heroin. I thought I was being really cool and nobody knew about it. Then Donald came up after the film was finished and said, there's one more shot to do, and inserted that one. It was him saying, I've got your number. So that was fun.'

W

Warner Bros

Film company that produced *Performance*.

Wet Dream Festival, The

A film festival dedicated to erotica, founded by Jim Haynes, sponsored by the alternative sex magazine *Suck*, and held in Amsterdam in the early Seventies. A ten-minute film of out-takes from the scenes of Jagger, Pallenberg and Breton tangling on the bed, entitled *Performance Trims*, was shown at the first festival in 1970, mostly consisting, Sandy Lieberson remembers, of 'Mick Jagger's cock and various parts of female anatomy'.

A columnist in the newspaper *Frij Nederlands* wrote that 'The revealed apparatus of the king of the Rolling Stones got much applause, but also disappointed people because Jagger's cock, of course, isn't any different from other cocks.'

The correspondent from *Paradiso Fox* apparently had his tape-measure to hand. 'For all those interested,' he wrote, 'Jagger has at least an 8-inch cock and full-bodied balls.'

Performance Trims was awarded the festival's Hung Jury Award. It is the only prize that *Performance* has ever won.

FILM CREDITS

Crew

Producer: Sanford Lieberson
Associate Producer: David Cammell
Production Manager: Robert Lyon
Unit Manager: Kevin Kavanagh
Director: Donald Cammell, Nicolas Roeg
Assistant Director: Richard Burge
Screenplay: Donald Cammell
Director of Photography: Nicolas Roeg
Camera Operator: Mike Molloy
Editor: Anthony Gibbs, Brian Smedley-Aston, Frank Mazzola
Art Director: John P. Clark
Set Dresser: Peter Young
Design Consultant for Turner's house: Christopher Gibbs
Costume Consultant: Deborah Dixon
Wardrobe: Emma Porteous, Billy Jay
Director of Authenticity: David Litvinoff
Music: Jack Nitzsche

Cast:

James Fox – Chas Devlin
Mick Jagger – Turner
Anita Pallenberg – Pherber

Michèle Breton – Lucy
Johnny Shannon – Harry Flowers
John Bindon – Moody
Stanley Meadows – Rosebloom
Ann Sidney – Dana
Anthony Valentine – Joey Maddocks
Allan Cuthbertson – the barrister, Harley-Brown
Anthony Morton – Dennis
Ken Colley – Tony Farrell
John Sterland – The chauffeur
Lorraine Wickens – Laraine

Production: Warner Bros Inc/A Goodtimes Enterprises
production Duration: 102 minutes.

ACKNOWLEDGEMENTS

Unless otherwise stated, all quotations in this book are from interviews conducted by the author. Portions of these interviews have previously appeared in the *Telegraph Magazine*.

I would like to thank Michèle Breton, David Cammell, Caroline Dawnay, James Fox, Christopher Gibbs, Myriam Gibril, Drew Hammond, Jim Haynes, Harvey Kubernick, Sandy Lieberson, Ruth Logan, Frank and Catherine Mazzola, George Melly, Kevin McDonald, Chris Rodley, Emma Soames, Claire Scobie, Johnny Shannon, Martin Sharp, Ann Sidney, Anita Pallenberg, Dick Polak, Caroline Upcher and Anthony Valentine. I am grateful to Norman Thomas di Giovanni for his advice, and for making available his hitherto unpublished translations of Jorge Luis Borges's short stories 'The South' and 'Tlon, Uqbar, Orbis Tertius'.

SELECTED BIBLIOGRAPHY

Borges, Jorge Luis, *Labyrinths*, Penguin, 1970.

Borges, Jorge Luis, *Collected Fictions*, Allen Lane the Penguin Press, 1999.

Cammell, C.R., *Aleister Crowley: The Black Magician*, New English Library, 1969.

Campbell, James, *The Beat Generation*, Secker & Warburg, 1999.

Cohn, Nik, *Ball the Wall, Nik Cohn in the Age of Rock* (ed. Gordon Burn), Picador, 1989.

Faithfull, Marianne, *Faithfull*, Michael Joseph, 1994.

Farber, Stephen, '*Performance*: The Nightmare Journey', *Cinema*, 1970.

Farson, Daniel, *The Gilded Gutter Life of Francis Bacon*, Century, 1993.

Fox, James, *Comeback*, Hodder and Stoughton, 1983.

Ford, Christopher, 'Nothing Queer about Johnny Shannon', *Guardian*, 1971.

Genet, Jean, *The Thief's Journal*, Anthony Blond, 1965.

Hayden-Guest, Anthony, 'She-Devil: The Lives and Loves of Anita Pallenberg', *Sunday Correspondent*, 1990.

Heinrich, Clark, *Strange Fruit: Alchemy, Religion and Magical Foods, A Speculative History*, Bloomsbury, 1995.

MacCabe, Colin, *Performance*, BFI Film Classics, 1998.

MacInnes, Colin, *Absolute Beginners*, MacGibbon & Kee, 1959.

Malcolm, Derek, 'What a Performance', *Guardian*, 1971.

Norman, Philip, *The Stones*, Hamish Hamilton, 1984.

Pearson, John, *The Profession of Violence*, Weidenfeld & Nicolson, 1972.

Savage, Jon, 'Tuning Into Wonders' (interview with Christopher Gibbs), *Sight & Sound*, 1995.

Time Out, *Performance* issue, 1970.

Scaduto, Anthony, *Mick Jagger*, W.H. Allen, 1974.

Wollen, Peter, 'Possession', *Sight & Sound*, 1995.

A NOTE ON THE AUTHOR

Mick Brown is the author of three previous books: *Richard Branson, The Inside Story, American Heartbeat: Travels from Woodstock to San Jose by Song Title*, and *The Spiritual Tourist*. Born in London in 1950, he is a freelance journalist and broadcaster.